新开端英语专业基础课系列教材

Extensive Reading

阅读拓展

Yuedu Tuozhan

4

总主编 胡 健 戚 涛
主 编 王 敏
副主编 朱蕴轶

学生用书
（第2版）

北京师范大学出版集团
BEIJING NORMAL UNIVERSITY PUBLISHING GROUP
安徽大学出版社

图书在版编目(CIP)数据

阅读拓展（4）学生用书 / 王敏主编 . -- 2 版 . -- 合肥：安徽大学出版社，2025.1
ISBN 978-7-5664-2804-2

Ⅰ.①阅… Ⅱ.①王… Ⅲ.①英语—阅读教学—高等学校—教材 Ⅳ.① H319.37

中国国家版本馆 CIP 数据核字（2024）第 023472 号

出版发行：	北京师范大学出版集团 安 徽 大 学 出 版 社 （安徽省合肥市肥西路 3 号 邮编 230039） www.bnupg.com www.ahupress.com.cn
印　　刷：	安徽利民印务有限公司
经　　销：	全国新华书店
开　　本：	880 mm × 1230 mm　1/16
印　　张：	15
字　　数：	449 千字
版　　次：	2025 年 1 月第 2 版
印　　次：	2025 年 1 月第 1 次印刷
定　　价：	49.90 元

ISBN 978-7-5664-2804-2

策划编辑：李　雪	装帧设计：李　军
责任编辑：李　雪	美术编辑：李　军
责任校对：高婷婷	责任印制：陈　如　孟献辉

版权所有　侵权必究

反盗版、侵权举报电话：0551-65106311
外埠邮购电话：0551-65107716
本书如有印装质量问题，请与印制管理部联系调换。
印制管理部电话：0551-65106311

前　言

在信息膨胀、知识爆炸的今天，面对数量庞大、纷繁芜杂的观点和信息，高效获取有价值的信息、辨识和评判各种观点，成了现代人的必备技能。因此，在高等英语教育中，提升学生的阅读能力，尤其是批判性阅读的能力成为了一项重要任务，这也对阅读教材的编写提出了更高的要求。作为英语专业的泛读教材，本教材在安徽省"十一五"规划教材《阅读拓展》（1~4册）的基础上进行修订。受时代因素所限，旧版教材存在文字相对陈旧、选材视野不宽、练习较为单调、缺乏思维训练等诸多缺憾。为应对国家培养复合型、创新型高素质英语人才的需求和AI时代提出的新挑战，本团队对旧版教材进行了大幅修改，其中第1册更新比例为70%，其余3册更新比例为100%。最突出的变化是：旧版教材局限在扩大词汇量及提高阅读能力；新版教材则着眼于阅读、批判性思维、跨文化交际、价值观等能力与素养的综合提升，尤其是第3、4册，突出了批判性阅读能力的训练。

教材第1、2册着重介绍英语阅读的常见技巧，旨在帮助学生在保证信息获取准确度的前提下，进一步提升阅读速度，从而提高阅读效率。第1、2册各8个单元，每单元有一个相对独立的主题，介绍一个主要的阅读技巧，包括快速获取主旨大意、通过上下文猜测词义、区分观点与事实等。

第1、2册每单元均分为Before Reading、While Reading、After Reading 3个部分。Before Reading部分起到课程导入的作用，形式丰富多样，有传统的课前讨论、词汇头脑风暴，也有新型的思维导图绘制及海报制作等。While Reading部分选材广泛，主题多样，涉及政治、经济、文化、环保、文学、社会等领域。所选文本长度与难度适中，一般为1000词左右，适合课堂教学及学生自学。文后配套练习的形式主

Extensive Reading 4

要包括阅读理解、判断正误、词汇配对、选词填空、读后讨论等，引导和帮助学生完成整个阅读过程。同时为了发挥"以读促写"的作用，部分单元还设计了相关的写作练习。After Reading 部分是学生深度思考和扩展知识的一个重要环节。此部分有扩展练习 Extension Exercise 和素养提升 Value Cultivation 等方面内容。Value Cultivation 每单元有不同主题，是传扬中国传统美德或其他类型价值正能量的课程思政内容，贴近学生的生活和学习，以"润物细无声"的方式帮助学生树立正确的人生观和世界观。此外，第1、2册还有机融入了跨文化交际意识和能力的培养。对于阅读文本中出现的文化差异、文化常识等内容均配有相应的注释或介绍，目的是在英语学习的基础阶段培养学生对跨文化交际的敏感性及对待文化差异的正确态度。

教材第3、4册在阅读技能提升的基础上，将批判性思维和课程思政融入英语阅读训练中，旨在帮助学生理解、分析和评判各种观点背后隐藏的逻辑，在此基础上学会选择与社会主义核心价值观相协调的价值立场。第3、4册各8个单元，内容涵盖批判性阅读的概念和相关理论、常用批判性阅读策略、基本论证类型和论证逻辑结构、逻辑推理知识以及常见逻辑谬误等，以阅读能力的提高为"驱动力"，旨在全面提升学生的批判性思维能力和英语综合应用能力，使学生能够对作者的观点、态度、假设、论证等进行分析、整合和评判，能够独立思考、提出问题、分析问题、解决问题。

第3、4册每个单元围绕1个批判性阅读相关概念或者策略展开，并提供2篇阅读材料。文章选自英语国家近年来出版的图书与网络材料，或节选自经典英文作品，其中很大一部分来自 BBC, *The Economist*, www.nytimes.com, *Time*, *The Washington Post*, *Scientific American* 等知名报刊杂志与网站，题材涉及教育、科技、语言、历史、艺术、文学、文化等诸多领域。文章均经过精挑细选，长度适中，难度相宜，少数地方做了必要的改写与删减。多数单元的理论介绍之后辅以巩固练习。每单元的两篇课文前均有 Preparatory Work 和课文导入，帮助学生调动图式背景，激发阅读兴趣，了解课文重点。文章后的 Notes 帮助学生了解文章背景和相关知识；文章后的练习根据 Bloom 教育目标分类表的 6 个层级，分为 Remembering and Understanding、Reasoning and Analyzing 和 Reflecting and Creating 3 个部分，并着重融入本单元的批判性阅读策略和技巧。3 个部分的练习内容丰富、形式活泼，主要有填空题、是非判断题、选择题、简答题、讨论题、画图题、短文写作等。单元最后有 3 个总结部分。Self-reflection 部分帮助学生反思本单元重难点的掌握情况。Value Cultivation 部分是课程思政内容，结合本单元话题，力求培养学生求真务实、开拓进取的治学态度和科学观，使学生具有高尚的道德情操、健全的人格、较高的人文素养；认同和坚持优秀的中华传统文化，具备辨别东西方文化中不同价值观的基本素质；具有党和国家意识以及社会主义核心价值观，既具有宽广的国际视野又具有爱国主义情怀。Further Reading 部分是拓展阅读推荐，供学生课后进一步拓展相关话题的阅读量和知识面。

  本套教材适合作为英语专业的教材，供第 1 至第 4 学期的教学使用，每学期 1 册。

  本次修订工作由安徽大学戚涛教授、胡健教授主持，全面负责教材的资料筛选、阅读技巧的编排、练习题型和题量的设定，以及定稿前的主审工作。教材编写具体分工如下：第 1 册张丽红老师编写第 1、5、7、8 单元，朱玲麟老师编写第 2、3、4、6 单元；第 2 册张丽红老师编写第 2、4、7、8 单元，朱玲麟老师编写第 1、3、5、6 单元；第 3 册朱蕴轶老师编写第 1、2、3、8 单元，王敏老师编写第 4、5、6、7 单元；第 4 册朱蕴轶老师编写第 1、4、5、8 单元，王敏老师编写第 2、3、6、7 单元。中国科技大学外籍教师 Murray Wayne Sherk 负责后期语言审校工作。

  虽然编写工作历时 2 年，编者也皆为从教多年的高校教师，但我们仍恐教材存在疏漏不妥之处，欢迎同行专家不吝赐教！

编 者

2024 年 7 月

★ CONTENTS ★

Unit 1 Classical Patterns of Arguments: Deduction 1
   Mastering Critical Reading 2
   Text A Declaration of Sentiments 6
   Text B A Room of One's Own (Excerpt) 18
   Summary 28

Unit 2 Classical Patterns of Arguments: Induction 31
   Mastering Critical Reading 32
   Text A How Art Movements Tried to Make Sense of the World
            in the Wake of the 1918 Flu Pandemic 36
   Text B Creative Thinking in Both Science
            and the Art Is Not for the Faint of Heart 46
   Summary 53

Unit 3 Aristotelian Model of Argument 57
   Mastering Critical Reading 58
   Text A Every Little Girl Wants to Be a Princess, Right? 61
   Text B I'm a Blind Scientist and Inventor.
            More Disabled Kids Should Have the Opportunities I Had 70
   Summary 77

Unit 4 Toulmin Model of Argument 81
   Mastering Critical Reading 82
   Text A Rising to the Occasion of Our Death 87

Text B In Defense of Voluntary Euthanasia 95
Summary 105

Unit 5 Nonrational Appeals 109

Mastering Critical Reading 110
Text A Antony's Funeral Oration (Excerpt) 115
Text B Animal Rights V. Animal Research: A Modest Proposal 131
Summary 139

Unit 6 Logical Fallacies 143

Mastering Critical Reading 144
Text A Love Is a Fallacy.. 150
Text B The Devious Art of Lying by Telling the Truth 165
Summary 172

Unit 7 Style 175

Mastering Critical Reading 176
Text A Why I Taught Myself to Procrastinate 181
Text B America Has a Love Affair with Exclamation Points! 190
Summary 198

Unit 8 Reading Literature Critically: Fiction 201

Mastering Critical Reading 202
Text A Lord of the Flies (Excerpt) 209
Text B The Oval Portrait 218
Summary 230

Unit 1
Classical Patterns of Arguments: Deduction

Extensive Reading 4

Mastering Critical Reading

There are two classical patterns of arguments: deduction and induction. Both refer to the process by which someone creates a conclusion and how they believe their conclusion to be true.

■ **What Is Deduction?**

(Source: https://www.jobtestsuccess.com/deductive-reasoning-test/)

Deduction (Latin for "lead down from") is the reasoning process requiring one to start with a few statements (premises), and apply them to a specific situation to reach a conclusion about the situation. Deduction does not give any new knowledge because the conclusion is extracted from the premises. In a deductively valid argument, if the premises are presumed to be true, the conclusion can't be false.

■ **Syllogism and Enthymeme**

In practice, the most basic form of deductive reasoning is **syllogism**, in which two statements—a major premise and a minor premise—are joined to produce a logical conclusion.

A classic example of syllogism:

Major premise: *All human beings are mortal.*

Minor premise: *Socrates is a human being.*

Conclusion: *Socrates is mortal.*

In the above syllogism, the major premise provides a general rule or principle that applies to all human beings. The minor premise applies a specific case to the general rule stated in the major premise. Since Socrates is a human being, and all human beings are mortal according to the major premise, it logically follows that Socrates must also be mortal.

Unit 1 Classical Patterns of Arguments: Deduction

Another example:

Major premise: *If demand exceeds supply, then prices increase.*
Minor premise: *Demand for oil has exceeded supply.*
Conclusion: *Therefore, oil prices will increase.*

In this example, the major premise is a conditional statement establishing a relationship between demand, supply, and prices. The minor premise states a specific instance where demand has surpassed supply for oil. So, the deductive reasoning in this syllogism is that if the two premises are true, the conclusion "Therefore, oil prices will increase" must also be true based on the established relationship between demand, supply, and prices.

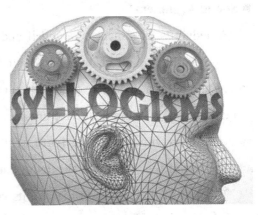

(Source: https://www.shutterstock.com/zh/search/syllogism)

Often a syllogism is incomplete with one of the premises or even the conclusion left unstated. The abbreviated syllogism is called **enthymeme**.

A classic example of enthymeme:

"He would not take the crown; Therefore 'tis certain he was not ambitious."

—William Shakespeare

In Shakespeare's *Julius Caesar*, Mark Antony delivers a funeral oration aiming to convince the audience that Caesar was not ambitious. One part of his argument is to highlight Caesar's refusal to accept the crown, using it as evidence to conclude that Caesar was, in fact, not ambitious. The statement "He would not take the crown; Therefore 'tis certain he was not ambitious" can be considered an enthymeme, as it contains an implicit premise. Here's the complete syllogism based on it:

Major Premise: *Ambitious people always seek positions of power and authority.*
Minor Premise: *Caesar refused the crown.*
Conclusion: *It is certain that Caesar was not ambitious.*

Another example:

"Circumstantial evidence can be very strong, as when you find a trout in the milk."

—Henry David Thoreau

In the argument, Thoreau only states the evidence that "there is a trout in the milk" while both the major premise and the conclusion remain implicit. Fully expressed, the argument turns into:

Major premise: *Trout live only in water.*
Minor premise: *The milk has a trout in it.*
Conclusion: *The milk is diluted with water.*

Extensive Reading 4

Obviously Thoreau in his witty remarks criticizes the farmers or grocers, who, in order to increase their profit, were known to dilute the milk with water.

■ **Sound Argument**

A deductive argument is sound if and only if it is both **valid**, and all of its premises are actually **true**. Otherwise, a deductive argument is unsound. In other words, a sound deductive argument has to pass two tests, **the test of the truth of premises and the test of the validity of the deduction**.

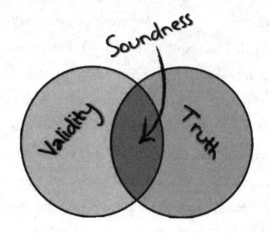

(Source: https://www.cantorsparadise.com/an-account-of-inductive-logic-and-deductive-logic-in-the-late-19th-century-6d8e115608a0)

The test of the premise relies on its **content**. The basic principle is to determine whether what it asserts corresponds with reality (e.g. There exist biological differences between men and women) or whether it is a shared value (e.g. In spite of the biological differences, men and women should enjoy equal pay for equal work); if it does, it is true; otherwise it is false. On the contrary, the validity of a deduction relies on its **form or logic**. The general principle for the test is to check whether the conclusion follows the premises: if one grants the premises, one must grant the conclusion.

Compare the following two syllogisms:

All musical instruments make sounds. *Airplanes make sounds.* *Therefore, airplanes are musical instruments.*	*All art is an imitation of nature.* *Music is art.* *Therefore, music is an imitation of nature.*

The syllogism on the left contains true premises. However, they don't guarantee the truth of the conclusion. Therefore, the argument is invalid. The syllogism on the right takes premises that overlap and uses them to prove that the conclusion is definitely true. Therefore, it is valid.

The validity of the two deductive arguments can be demonstrated more clearly like this:

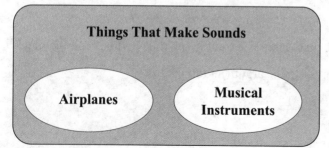
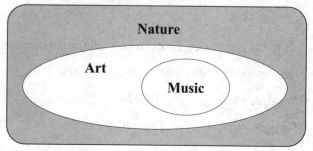

Unit 1 Classical Patterns of Arguments: Deduction

■ Typical Forms of Valid Arguments

Example	Form
All organisms have RNA. This fruit fly is an organism. Therefore, this fruit fly has RNA.	All A are B; C is A; Therefore, C is B.
If John is ill, then he won't be able to attend our meeting today. John is ill. Therefore, John won't be able to attend our meeting today.	If A, then B; A; Therefore, B.
No cowards can be great leaders. Falstaff was a coward. Falstaff was not a great leader.	No A are B; C is A; Therefore, C is not B.
If Kelly does not finish his homework, he will not go to class. Kelly went to school. Therefore, Kelly had finished his homework.	If A, then B; Not B; Therefore, not A.

🔑 Enhancing Your Critical Reading

Activity 1 Make a Syllogism

Try to make a complete syllogism out of the following dialogue.

A: Did you hear about Jean's father? He had a heart attack last week.

B: That's too bad. But I'm not surprised. I know he always refused to go for his annual physical checkups.

Major premise:	
Minor premise:	
Conclusion:	

Activity 2 Make a Judgement

Determine whether the following are sound arguments or not.

Deductive Argument	Sound/Unsound
All organisms have RNA. *This fruit fly is an organism.* *Therefore, this fruit fly has RNA.*	True and Valid—Sound
All items made of gold are time-travel devices. *This toaster is made of gold.* *Therefore, this toaster is a time-travel device.*	

Extensive Reading 4

(continued)

Deductive Argument	Sound/Unsound
All Americans prefer vanilla ice cream to other flavors. Tiger Woods prefers vanilla ice cream to other flavors. Therefore, Tiger Woods is an American.	
All basketballs are round. The Earth is round. Therefore, the Earth is a basketball.	
If the temperature is below freezing, then water will freeze. The water is frozen. Therefore, the temperature is below freezing.	
No birds are mammals. Penguins are birds. Therefore, penguins are not mammals.	
If you study diligently, then you will pass the exam. You do not study diligently. Therefore, you will not pass the exam.	

Text A Declaration of Sentiments

Preparatory Work

Activity 1 Brainstorming: Word Association

(Source: https://equineteurope.org/equality-matters-sexism/)

What does the word "equality" mean? Brainstorm as many related words or phrases as you can. Make connections to your prior knowledge or personal experiences. Share and discuss your ideas as a class, highlighting key concepts that came up.

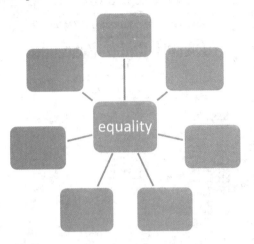

Activity 2 Learn about the First Women's Rights Convention

(Stanton read the document at the convention on July 20th, 1848, Source: https://www.mediastorehouse.com.au/granger-art-on-demand/womens-rights-convention-elizabeth-cady-stanton-7505255.html)

(Source: https://amazingwomeninhistory.com/seneca-falls-convention-summary-and-significance/)

Extensive Reading 4

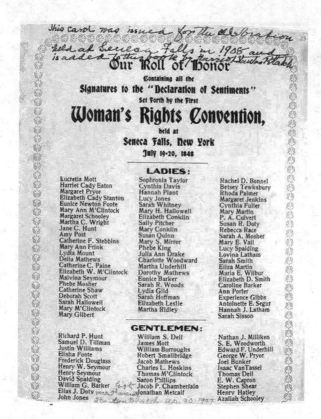

(Signers of the Declaration of Sentiments at Seneca Falls, Source: https://en.wikipedia.org/wiki/Declaration_of_Sentiments)

Look at the pictures about the First Women's Rights Convention/Seneca Falls Convention. Do some research about the Convention based on the following questions and then have a discussion in small groups.

❖ When and where was the First Women's Rights Convention held?

❖ Who organized the convention and why was the convention organized?

❖ What is the key issue addressed in the convention?

❖ How many people signed the document?

❖ What were some of the barriers faced by women in the 19th century that the convention sought to address?

❖ How did the First Women's Rights Convention contribute to the broader women's rights movement in the United States?

Reading the Text

> The "Declaration of Sentiments", published in 1848 at the Seneca Falls Convention on women's rights, is considered a founding document of the women's rights movement. It is one of the early public documents advocating for full civil rights for women, including the right to vote.

Declaration of Sentiments[1]
Elizabeth Cady Stanton[2]

1 When, in the course of human events, it becomes necessary for one portion of the family of man to assume among the people of the earth a position different from that which they have hitherto occupied, but one to which the laws of nature and of nature's God entitle them, a decent respect to the opinions of mankind requires that they should declare the causes that impel them to such a course.

2 We hold these truths to be self-evident; that all men and women are created equal; that they are endowed by their Creator with certain inalienable rights; that among these are life, liberty, and the pursuit of happiness; that to secure these rights governments are instituted, deriving their just powers from the consent of the governed. Whenever any form of government becomes destructive of these ends, it is the right of those who suffer from it to refuse allegiance to it, and to insist upon the institution of a new government, laying its foundation on such principles, and organizing its powers in such form as to them shall seem most likely to effect their safety and happiness. Prudence, indeed, will dictate that governments long established should not be changed for light and transient causes; and accordingly, all experience hath shown that mankind are more disposed to suffer, while evils are sufferable, than to right themselves by abolishing the forms to which they were accustomed. But when a long train of abuses and usurpations, pursuing invariably the same object, evinces a design to reduce them under absolute despotism, it is their duty to throw off such government, and to provide new guards for their future security. Such has been the patient sufferance of the women under this government, and such is now the necessity which constrains them to demand the equal station to which they are entitled.

3 The history of mankind is a history of repeated injuries and usurpations on the part of man toward woman, having in direct object the establishment of an absolute tyranny over her. To prove this, let facts be submitted to a candid world.

4 He has never permitted her to exercise her inalienable right to the elective franchise.

5 He has compelled her to submit to laws, in the formation of which she had no voice.

Extensive Reading 4

(Declaration of Sentiments-100 Women Trailblazers, Source: https://www.britannica.com/explore/100women/about-suffragist-movement/declaration-of-sentiments)

6   He has withheld from her rights which are given to the most ignorant and degraded men—both natives and foreigners.

7   Having deprived her of this first right of a citizen, the elective franchise, thereby leaving her without representation in the halls of legislation, he has oppressed her on all sides.

8   He has made her, if married, in the eye of the law, civilly dead.

9   He has taken from her all right in property, even to the wages she earns.

10 He has made her, morally, an irresponsible being, as she can commit many crimes, with impunity, provided they be done in the presence of her husband. In the covenant of marriage, she is compelled to promise obedience to her husband, he becoming, to all intents and purposes, her master—the law giving him power to deprive her of her liberty, and to administer chastisement.

(Elizabeth Cady Stanton addressing the Senate Committee on Privileges and Elections, Washington, D.C. from the New York Daily Graphic, January 16th, 1878. Source: https://www.nyhistory.org/blogs/the-declaration-of-sentiments-no-more-or-less-radical-than-the-american-revolution)

¹¹ He has so framed the laws of divorce, as to what shall be the proper causes of divorce, in case of separation, to whom the guardianship of the children shall be given; as to be wholly regardless of the happiness of women—the law, in all cases, going upon the false supposition of the supremacy of man, and giving all power into his hands.

¹² After depriving her of all rights as a married woman, if single and the owner of property, he has taxed her to support a government which recognizes her only when her property can be made profitable to it.

¹³ He has monopolized nearly all the profitable employments, and from those she is permitted to follow, she receives but a scanty remuneration.

¹⁴ He closes against her all the avenues to wealth and distinction, which he considers most honorable to himself. As a teacher of theology, medicine, or law, she is not known.

¹⁵ He has denied her the facilities for obtaining a thorough education—all colleges being closed against her.

¹⁶ He allows her in Church as well as State, but a subordinate position, claiming Apostolic authority for her exclusion from the ministry, and with some exceptions, from any public participation in the affairs of the Church.

¹⁷ He has created a false public sentiment, by giving to the world a different code of morals for men and women by which moral delinquencies which exclude women from society, are not only tolerated but deemed of little account in man.

¹⁸ He has usurped the prerogative of Jehovah himself, claiming it as his right to assign for her a sphere of action, when that belongs to her conscience and her God.

¹⁹ He has endeavored, in every way that he could to destroy her confidence in her own powers, to lessen her self-respect, and to make her willing to lead a dependent and abject life.

(Source: https://americanliterature.com/history/elizabeth-cady-stanton/declaration/the-declaration-of-sentiments)

Extensive Reading 4

[20] Now, in view of this entire disfranchisement of one-half the people of this country, their social and religious degradation—in view of the unjust laws above mentioned, and because women do feel themselves aggrieved, oppressed, and fraudulently deprived of their most sacred rights, we insist that they have immediate admission to all the rights and privileges which belong to them as citizens of these United States.

[21] In entering upon the great work before us, we anticipate no small amount of misconception, misrepresentation, and ridicule; but we shall use every instrumentality within our power to effect our object. We shall employ agents, circulate tracts, petition the State and national Legislatures, and endeavor to enlist the pulpit and the press in our behalf. We hope this Convention will be followed by a series of Conventions, embracing every part of the country.

(Source: The text is available at https://www.nps.gov/wori/learn/historyculture/declaration-of-sentiments.htm)

Notes

1. The **"Declaration of Sentiments"** is a document deliberately patterned after the "Declaration of Independence" and delivered at the **First Women's Rights Convention.** On July 9th, 1848, five reform-minded women (Elizabeth Cady Stanton, Lucretia Mottmet, Martha Coffin Wright, Mary Ann M'Clintock and Jane Hunt) at a social gathering in Waterloo, New York and decided to hold a convention, a very common way to promote change in 1848. They published a "call" in the local newspaper inviting people to "a Convention to discuss the social, civil and religious rights and condition of woman". The convention was held on July 19th and 20th in Seneca Falls, New York. Relying heavily on pre-existing networks of reformers, relatives, and friends, the convention drew over 300 people. "The Declaration of Sentiments" was read by Stanton at the Seneca Falls Convention on July 20, and eventually one hundred participants including sixty-eight women and thirty-two men signed the document.

2. **Elizabeth Cady Stanton** (1815–1902) was an American leader in the women's rights movement, who in 1848 formulated the first concerted demand for women's suffrage in the United States.

Unit 1 Classical Patterns of Arguments: Deduction

 Remembering and Understanding

Activity 1 Answer the Following Questions

1. According to the text, when is it necessary for one portion of the family of man to assume a different position among the people of the earth?

   _____
   _____

2. What rights are mentioned as being endowed to all men and women by their Creator?

   _____
   _____

3. What is the right of those who suffer from a destructive government?

   _____
   _____

4. Why does the author state that governments should not be changed for light and transient causes?

   _____
   _____

5. What is meant by "he" in the "Declaration of Sentiments"?

   _____
   _____

6. How does the author describe the treatment of women in marriage?

   _____
   _____

7. What is the position of women in society and the church, according to the text?

   _____
   _____

8. What are the actions of men in relation to women's rights and self-confidence?

   _____
   _____

9. What strategies are mentioned for achieving the objective stated in the text?

   _____
   _____

Activity 2 Outline the Grievances in the "Declaration of Sentiments"

From Para. 4 to Para. 19, the text lists 16 abusive laws and practices that violated women's natural rights at

Extensive Reading 4

the hands of men. Outline the 16 grievances and identify the corresponding paragraphs.

Categories of the Grievances	Corresponding Paragraphs
1. Denial of political rights and representation	Para. 4 - Para. 7
2.	
3.	
4.	
5.	
6.	

Reasoning and Analyzing

Activity 1 Multiple-choice Questions

Choose the best answer from the four choices given based on the text.

1. What is the significance of the phrase "all men and women are created equal" in the "Declaration of Sentiments"?

    A. It highlights the need for women to become superior to men.

    B. It acknowledges the natural rights and equality of both genders.

    C. It promotes the idea that men are superior to women.

    D. It argues that women should not have the same rights as men.

2. Which of the following is closest in meaning to "prerogative" in "He has usurped the prerogative of Jehovah himself" (Para. 18)?

    A. Privilege.   B. Obligation.

    C. Prohibition.   D. Exemption.

3. The main purpose of the "Declaration of Sentiments" is to _____.

    A. declare independence from Great Britain

    B. demand equality for women in education and employment

    C. address the inequalities and injustices faced by women

Unit 1 Classical Patterns of Arguments: Deduction

D. promote religious freedom

4. Which of the following best demonstrates the use of deductive reasoning in the "Declaration of Sentiments"?

   A. It argues that because women are created equal to men and possess the same inherent rights, they should be granted the same rights as men.

   B. It asserts that women have been historically oppressed and denied their basic rights; therefore, they must fight for their equality and recognition.

   C. It states that since women have the ability to reason and possess a moral conscience, they should be allowed to participate in all aspects of society, including politics.

   D. It claims that women's subordinate status in society has persisted for centuries; hence, they must take collective action and demand change.

5. The tone of the "Declaration of Sentiments" can be best described as _____.

   A. submissive and apologetic   B. angry and confrontational

   C. objective and informative   D. persuasive and empowering

Activity 2 Identify and analyze the central deductive argument in the "Declaration of Sentiments" based on the following questions.

1. What is the central deductive argument in the "Declaration of Sentiments"? State the argument in syllogistic form consisting of major premise, minor premise, and conclusion. Construct a valid argument.

   _____
   _____

2. How is the major premise composed? Which paragraphs are devoted to supporting the major premise? What kind of support is given?

   _____
   _____

3. How is the minor premise composed? Which paragraphs are devoted to supporting the minor premise? What kind of support is given?

   _____
   _____

4. Which premise is given more support? And why?

   _____
   _____

Extensive Reading 4

🔖 Reflecting and Creating

Activity 1 Reflect and Discuss

(Suffragettes parade through New York City. https://www.businessinsider.com/womens-rights-suffragettes-voting-election-vintage-photos)

❖ Choose a statement or complaint included in the "Declaration of Sentiments".
❖ Share the quote chosen in small groups and explain what this means in your own words.
❖ How does this statement or complaint relate to the events and ideas that contributed to the Seneca Falls Convention?
❖ Is this specific statement or complaint still applicable today? Give examples to illustrate your point.

Activity 2 Compare and Evaluate

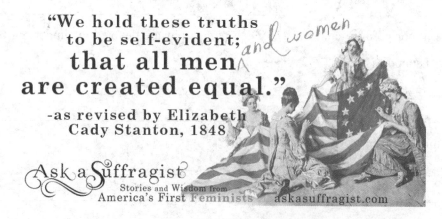

(Source: https://askasuffragist.com/tag/elizabeth-cady-stanton/)

Unit 1 Classical Patterns of Arguments: Deduction

The "Declaration of Sentiments" by Elizabeth Cady Stanton at that time was closely modeled on the framework of the "Declaration of Independence" which was ratified on July 4, 1776, proclaiming the independence of the thirteen American colonies from Great Britain. Make a comparative study of the two documents.

❖ Highlight typical differences between them.

❖ Write a paragraph to evaluate how the "Declaration of Sentiments" achieves its purposes through such differences.

Declaration of Sentiments	Declaration of Independence
1. We hold these truths to be self-evident; that all men *and women* are created equal.	1. We hold these truths to be self-evident; that all men are created equal.

Extensive Reading 4

Text B A Room of One's Own (Excerpt)

Preparatory Work

Activity 1 Women in Literature

(Source: https://classicbookreader.wordpress.com/2013/09/17/20-most-influential-women-authors-of-all-time/)

Discuss in small groups and fill out the box based on the following questions:

❖ Do you know any women writers in history?

❖ What is your favorite work written by them?

❖ What is the book mainly about? Can you tell whether a work is written by a male or female before knowing its author? If yes, how to tell the difference?

❖ What do you think of the impact of women's writing on literature?

Women in Literature	
Women Writers I Know	
My Favorite Work Written by Women	
What the Book Is about	
The Difference between Men's and Women's Writing	
The Impact of Women Literature	

Activity 2 A Research on Feminism

(Source: https://www.abc.net.au/btn/high/what-is-feminism/102063904)

What do you know about feminism? Do some research or make connections to your prior knowledge to fill out the missing information in the box.

Feminism	
Definition of Feminism	
Different Types of Feminism	

Extensive Reading 4

(continued)

Feminism	
Famous Feminists and Their Representative Works	
Four Waves of Feminist Movements	
Impact of the Movements	

Reading the Text

> "Cats do not go heaven. Women cannot write the plays of Shakespeare."[1] Is this ridiculous or a matter-of-fact? Woolf addresses the limitations that past and present women writers face by arguing "A woman must have money and a room of her own if she is to write fiction".

A Room of One's Own[2]

(Excerpt)

Virginia Woolf[3]

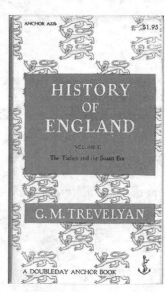

(Source: https://www.amazon.com/History-England-G-M-Trevelyan/dp/0385092903)

1 I went, therefore, to the shelf where the histories stand and took down one of the latest, Professor Trevelyan's *History of England*[4]. Once more I looked up "Women", found "position of" and turned to the pages indicated. "Wife–beating", I read, "was a recognized right of man, and was practised without shame by high as well as low... Similarly," the historian goes on, "the daughter who refused to marry the gentleman of her parents' choice was liable to be locked up, beaten and flung about the room, without any shock being inflicted on public opinion. Marriage was not an affair of personal affection, but of family avarice, particularly in the 'chivalrous' upper classes... Betrothal often took place while one or both of the parties was in the cradle, and marriage when they were scarcely out of the nurses' charge." That was about 1470, soon after Chaucer's time[5]. The next reference to the position of women is some two hundred years later, in the time of the Stuarts.[6] "It was still the exception

for women of the upper and middle class to choose their own husbands, and when the husband had been assigned, he was lord and master, so far at least as law and custom could make him. Yet even so," Professor Trevelyan concludes, "neither Shakespeare's women nor those of authentic seventeenth–century memoirs… seem wanting in personality and character." … Indeed, if woman had no existence save in the fiction written by men, one would imagine her a person of the utmost importance; very various; heroic and mean; splendid and sordid; infinitely beautiful and hideous in the extreme; as great as a man, some think even greater. But this is woman in fiction. In fact, as Professor Trevelyan points out, she was locked up, beaten and flung about the room.

2 A very queer, composite being thus emerges. Imaginatively she is of the highest importance; practically she is completely insignificant. She pervades poetry from cover to cover; she is all but absent from history…

3 …It would be ambitious beyond my daring, I thought, looking about the shelves for books that were not there, to suggest to the students of those famous colleges that they should rewrite history, though I own that it often seems a little queer as it is, unreal, lop–sided; but why should they not add a supplement to history, calling it, of course, by some inconspicuous name so that women might figure there without impropriety? …Here am I asking why women did not write poetry in the Elizabethan age[7], and I am not sure how they were educated; whether they were taught to write; whether they had sitting–rooms to themselves; how many women had children before they were twenty–one; what, in short, they did from eight in the morning till eight at night. They had no money evidently; according to Professor Trevelyan they were married whether they liked it or not before they were out of the nursery, at fifteen or sixteen very likely. It would have been extremely odd, even upon this showing, had one of them suddenly written the plays of Shakespeare, I concluded, and I thought of that old gentleman, who is dead now, but was a bishop, I think, who declared that it was impossible for any woman, past, present, or to come, to have the genius of Shakespeare. He wrote to the papers about it. He also told a lady who applied to him for information that cats do not as a matter of fact go to heaven, though they have, he added, souls of a sort. How much thinking those old gentlemen used to save one! How the borders of ignorance shrank back at their approach! Cats do not go to heaven. Women cannot write the plays of Shakespeare.

(Source: https://www.facebook.com/VWSGB/photos/819776131461799/?locale=pt_BR)

Extensive Reading 4

4   Be that as it may, I could not help thinking, as I looked at the works of Shakespeare on the shelf, that the bishop was right at least in this; it would have been impossible, completely and entirely, for any woman to have written the plays of Shakespeare in the age of Shakespeare. Let me imagine, since facts are so hard to come by, what would have happened had Shakespeare had a wonderfully gifted sister, called Judith, let us say. Shakespeare himself went, very probably—his mother was an heiress—to the grammar school, where he may have learnt Latin—Ovid, Virgil and Horace[8]—and the elements of grammar and logic. He was, it is well known, a wild boy who poached rabbits, perhaps shot a deer, and had, rather sooner than he should have done, to marry a woman in the neighbourhood, who bore him a child rather quicker than was right. That escapade sent him to seek his fortune in London. He had, it seemed, a taste for the theatre; he began by holding horses at the stage door. Very soon he got work in the theatre, became a successful actor, and lived at the hub of the universe, meeting everybody, knowing everybody, practising his art on the boards, exercising his wits in the streets, and even getting access to the palace of the queen. Meanwhile his extraordinarily gifted sister, let us suppose, remained at home. She was as adventurous, as imaginative, as agog to see the world as he was. But she was not sent to school. She had no chance of learning grammar and logic, let alone of reading Horace and Virgil. She picked up a book now and then, one of her brother's perhaps, and read a few pages. But then her parents came in and told her to mend the stockings or mind the stew and not moon about with books and papers. They would have spoken sharply but kindly, for they were substantial people who knew the conditions of life for a woman and loved their daughter—indeed, more likely than not she was the apple of her father's eye. Perhaps she scribbled some pages up in an apple loft on the sly but was careful to hide them or set fire to them. Soon, however, before she was out of her teens, she was to be betrothed to the son of a neighbouring woolstapler. She cried out that marriage was hateful to her, and for that she was severely beaten by her father. Then he ceased to scold her. He begged her instead not to hurt him, not to shame him in this matter of her marriage. He would give her a chain of beads or a fine petticoat, he said; and there were tears in his eyes. How could she disobey him? How could she break his heart? The force of her own gift alone drove her to it. She made up a small parcel of her belongings, let herself down by a rope one summer's night and took the road to London. She was not seventeen. The birds that sang in the hedge were not more musical than she was. She had the quickest fancy, a gift like her brother's, for the tune of words. Like him, she had a taste for the theatre. She stood at the stage door; she wanted to act, she said. Men laughed in her face. The manager—a fat, looselipped man—guffawed. He bellowed something about poodles dancing and women acting—no woman, he said, could possibly be an actress. He hinted—you can imagine what. She could get no training in her craft. Could she even seek her dinner in a tavern or roam the streets at midnight? Yet her genius was for fiction and lusted to feed abundantly upon the lives of men and women and the study of their ways. At last—for she was very young, oddly like Shakespeare the poet in her face, with the same

grey eyes and rounded brows—at last Nick Greene the actor manager took pity on her; she found herself with child by that gentleman and so—who shall measure the heat and violence of the poet's heart when caught and tangled in a woman's body?—killed herself one winter's night and lies buried at some crossroads where the omnibuses now stop outside the Elephant and Castle[9].

(Source: https://kayiprihtim.com/liste/virginia-woolf-hakkinda-bilgi/)

5 …This may be true or it may be false—who can say? —But what is true in it, so it seemed to me, reviewing the story of Shakespeare's sister as I had made it, is that any woman born with a great gift in the sixteenth century would certainly have gone crazed, shot herself, or ended her days in some lonely cottage outside the village, half witch, half wizard, feared and mocked at. For it needs little skill in psychology to be sure that a highly gifted girl who had tried to use her gift for poetry would have been so thwarted and hindered by other people, so tortured and pulled asunder by her own contrary instincts, that she must have lost her health and sanity to a certainty. …To have lived a free life in London in the sixteenth century would have meant for a woman who was poet and playwright a nervous stress and dilemma which might well have killed her. Had she survived, whatever she had written would have been twisted and deformed, issuing from a strained and morbid imagination. And undoubtedly, I thought, looking at the shelf where there are no plays by women, her work would have gone unsigned. That refuge she would have sought certainly. It was the relic of the sense of chastity that dictated anonymity to women even so late as the nineteenth century.

(Source: The text is abridged from Chapter Three of *A Room of One's Own* published by Martino Fine Books, reprint edition, 2012)

Extensive Reading 4

Notes

1. **William Shakespeare** (1564-1616), an iconic English playwright, poet and actor, is widely regarded as one of the greatest writers in the English language. His body of work includes 39 plays, 154 sonnets, and some other poems. Some of his most famous plays include *Romeo and Juliet, Hamlet, Macbeth, Othello*, and *A Midsummer Night's Dream*. Shakespeare's works have had a profound impact on literature, theatre, and culture.

2. *A Room of One's Own* is an extended essay consisting of six chapters, based on Woolf's lectures at Cambridge University in 1928. In it, Woolf addresses her thoughts on "the question of women and fiction". Her chief standing on it is "a woman must have money and a room of her own if she is to write fiction". The text is abridged from Chapter Three.

3. **Virginia Woolf** (1882-1941), a famous English novelist, essayist, critic, and feminist, was one of the foremost leaders of the literary movement of Modernism. As a novelist, Woolf's primary was not on plot or characterization but on characters' consciousness, their thoughts and feelings, which she brilliantly illuminated by the stream of consciousness technique. Her most famous novels include *Mrs. Dalloway* (1925), *To the Lighthouse* (1927) and *Orlando* (1928).

4. **George Macaulay Trevelyan** (1876-1962) was a British historian and author known for his influential works on British history. He served as a professor at the University of Cambridge, and was a member of the famous Trevelyan family. Some of his well-known works include *History of England* and *English Social History*. First published in 1926, ***History of England*** provides a detailed and comprehensive account of the history of England from the Roman era to the early 20th century.

5. **Geoffrey Chaucer** (1340s-1400), the "father of English literature", is considered one of the greatest English poets of the Middle Ages and best known for his work, ***The Canterbury Tales***. Chaucer's time saw significant social, political, and cultural changes, including the transition from the medieval to the Renaissance period, and the rise of the English language as a literary medium.

6. The time of the **Stuarts** refers to the period when the Stuart dynasty ruled England, Scotland, and Ireland from 1603 to 1714. It is named after the ruling family, which included James I, Charles I, Charles II, James II, William III, and Mary II, Anne. This era was marked by political and religious strife, including the English Civil War (1642-1651), the Glorious Revolution (1688), and the Jacobite Risings in Scotland.

7. **The Elizabethan Age,** also known as the Elizabethan Era, refers to the period of English history during the reign of Queen Elizabeth I, which lasted from 1558 to 1603. It is known for its cultural and artistic advancements, as well as its political stability and economic prosperity.

8. **Ovid, Virgil, and Horace** are three Roman poets who were active during the golden age of Latin literature in the 1st century BC. Ovid is best known for his epic poem, *Metamorphoses*. Virgil's most famous work is the epic poem, *Aeneid*. Horace is known for his lyric poetry and his influential collection of odes, *Odes*. They made significant contributions to Latin literature and played a crucial role in shaping the literary tradition of ancient Rome.

9. **Elephant and Castle** is the name of a pub/coaching inn located at this major crossroad.

Unit 1 Classical Patterns of Arguments: Deduction

 Remembering and Understanding

Activity 1 Identify and Synthesize information

At the beginning of the essay, Woolf gives a description of the practices towards women in the past based on Professor Trevelyan's History of England. *Fill out the missing information according to your understanding of the first paragraph.*

Practices towards Women Indicated in History of England	
❖ About 1470, Soon after Chaucer's Time	
❖ The Time of the Stuarts	
❖ Women in Fictions	
❖ Women Described by Prof. Trevelyan	

In Para. 4, Woolf imagines a hypothetical scenario of Shakespeare having a gifted sister named Judith. Fill out the missing information based on your understanding of the paragraph.

Shakespeare and His Fictional Sister, Judith Shakespeare	
The Same Traits They Exhibit	
The Innate Difference Between Them	
The Difference Between Their Lives	

Activity 2 True or False Questions

Are the following statements true or false? Make your decisions based on the text.

(   ) 1. During the time of the Stuarts in England, it was common for women of the upper and middle classes to have the freedom to choose their own husbands.

(   ) 2. In Shakespeare's plays and authentic seventeenth-century memoirs, women were depicted as

Extensive Reading 4

lacking personality and character.

(　　) 3. Professor Trevelyan suggests that women portrayed in fiction written by men are often depicted as important and diverse individuals.

(　　) 4. The author suggests that history should be rewritten to include the contributions of women in a supplement.

(　　) 5. The author agrees with the bishop who believes that women cannot possess the same genius as Shakespeare.

(　　) 6. According to the passage, it would have been impossible for any woman to have written the plays of Shakespeare in his time.

(　　) 7. Shakespeare's sister, Judith, wasn't sent to school and had no opportunity to learn grammar and logic because the family was poor.

(　　) 8. Because her father didn't love her at all, Judith was severely beaten by him when she refused the arranged marriage.

(　　) 9. Judith disobeyed her father and ran away to London to pursue her dream of acting.

(　　) 10. Judith's story suggests highly gifted women in the 16th century would have faced societal pressure and constraints that would have ultimately led to their insanity or demise.

Reasoning and Analyzing

Activity 1　Multiple-choice Questions

Choose the best answer from the four choices given based on the text.

1. What does the author imply by "A very queer, composite being" (Para. 2)?

    A. Women are important in poetry but absent in history.

    B. Women are important in both poetry and history.

    C. Women are absent in both poetry and history.

    D. Women are important in history but absent in poetry.

2. Why does the author believe it would be ambitious to suggest rewriting history to include women?

    A. It would be inappropriate to include women in history.

    B. Women's contributions to history are insignificant.

    C. The author doubts that women were educated or had opportunities to write.

    D. Women's presence in history was intentionally concealed.

3. Woolf's tone can be best summarized as _____ in "Cats do not go to heaven. Women cannot write the plays of Shakespeare".

    A. sympathetic　　　　B. sarcastic　　　　C. humorous　　　　D. cautious

4. A highly gifted girl born in the sixteenth century would have faced challenges and potentially lost her health and sanity because _____.

   A. she would have been ridiculed and mocked for her talents

   B. society at the time did not value women's intellectual pursuits

   C. her own conflicting instincts and societal expectations would have caused distress

   D. writing poetry and pursuing a career in London would have been physically demanding

5. According to the text, why would a woman writer in the sixteenth century likely choose to remain anonymous?

   A. Women were not allowed to publish under their own names.

   B. Writers at the time preferred to keep their identities a secret.

   C. It was a convention for all writers, regardless of gender, to remain anonymous.

   D. Anonymity would protect the writer's reputation and chastity.

Activity 2 Analyze the Deductive Reasoning

In the abridged text, Woolf argues, based on the tragic story of Judith, Shakespeare's fictional sister, women in the sixteenth century, despite being imaginative and talented, would have been hindered, marginalized, and potentially driven to madness or even death by societal expectations and limitations. Use the following questions to help you work out the premises in the author's deduction about Judith's downfall.

- What evidence from the historical context and societal norms of the sixteenth century does the author use to deduce the fate of Judith?
- How does the author establish the premise that Judith is equally imaginative and talented as Shakespeare?
- How does the hypothetical scenario of Judith's life help explore the societal constraints on women during the sixteenth century?
- Is there any specific textual evidence that directly supports the author's deduction about Judith's downfall?

Woolf's Deduction about Judith's Tragic End	
Premises	
Conclusion	It is unlikely that Judith Shakespeare would have been able to write plays like her brother.
Premises	
Conclusion	Therefore, Judith Shakespeare would have been hindered, marginalized, and potentially driven to madness or even death.

Extensive Reading 4

Reflecting and Creating

Activity 1 Topics for Discussion and Writing

1. Woolf argues writers like Shakespeare could not have been born among women in his time. Do you agree with the author? Or do you think women were capable of producing, and in fact free to produce, work of the quality of William Shakespeare? Exchange your views in small groups.

2. Woolf suggests that history should be rewritten to include the contributions of women in a supplement because "nothing is known about women before the eighteenth century". Do you think it was the same situation for women in ancient China? Write a short essay about Chinese women's position and their contributions in history.

Activity 2 Create "A Room of One's Own"

Everyone needs "a room of one's own" for rest, meditation, reflection, reading or writing. Share your ideas as a class based on the following questions:

- Do you have "a room of one's own"? If not, brainstorm strategies about how you would go about creating this solitary space.
- Where could you go to concentrate?
- Where could you go for inspiration?
- What would you do in "a room of one's own"?
- If you were to write in this room, what would you want to write?
- Would you need a computer or would you use a pen and paper?

(Source: https://www.virginiawoolfproject.com/a-room-of-ones-own-by-virginia-woolf-1929/)

Summary

 Self-reflection

Fill out the checklist.

Area	Yes/No?	Notes/Comment
I know what deduction is.		

(continued)

Area	Yes/No?	Notes/Comment
I know the typical form of deductive arguments is syllogism which consists of a major premise, a minor premise and a conclusion.		
I know an enthymeme is a compressed syllogism.		
I know how to make a syllogism out of an enthymeme.		
I know the typical forms of valid arguments.		
I know the two principles that make a sound argument.		
I know how to evaluate a deductive argument.		

Value Cultivation

Activity 1 Quote Sharing

Translate the quotes either in English or Chinese and explain them in your own words.

1. 在中国人民追求美好生活的过程中，每一位妇女都有人生出彩和梦想成真的机会。中国将更加积极贯彻男女平等基本国策，发挥妇女"半边天"作用，支持妇女建功立业、实现人生理想和梦想。中国妇女也将通过自身发展不断促进世界妇女运动发展，为全球男女平等事业作出更大贡献。

——习近平总书记在全球妇女峰会上的讲话

2. 要做一个比较有批判力的女性主义者，不能仅仅做一个激进的女性主义者，不能只是去批判男人，因为男人也是社会性别制度的一部分；应该在一种更开放、更广阔的视野中去讨论女性问题。既要讨论父权制，又要讨论社会制度，或者说组织资本和劳动的社会制度。

——贺桂梅

3. Anon, who wrote so many poems without signing them, was often a woman.

—Virginia Woolf

4. One is not born, but rather becomes, a woman.

—Simone de Beauvoir

Extensive Reading 4

Activity 2 Group Discussion: How to Encompass the Full Range of Human Emotions and Experiences

Woolf concludes in *A Room of One's Own* by arguing that in fact, an ideal writer should be neither narrowly "male" nor "female" but instead should strive to be emotionally and psychologically androgynous in their approach to gender. In other words, writers should write with an understanding of both masculinity and femininity, rather than writing "merely" as a woman or as a man. This will allow writers to encompass the full range of human emotions and experiences. Do you agree with Woolf's androgynous approach in writing? Share your opinions in small groups regarding the strategies we can take to encompass the full range of human emotions and experiences regardless of gender, race, age, culture, ideology, etc.

Further Reading

1. 《女性文学与性别政治的变迁》——贺桂梅
2. 《促进妇女全面发展　共建共享美好世界》——习近平总书记在全球妇女峰会上的讲话
3. *A Room of One's Own* by Virginia Woolf
4. *The Second Sex* by Simone de Beauvoir

Unit 2
Classical Patterns of Arguments: Induction

Extensive Reading 4

Mastering Critical Reading

Induction, like deduction, is an essential form of reasoning. However, in contrast to deduction reasoning, inductive reasoning works the other way in reaching conclusions and differs in certainty about the conclusions.

■ **What Is Induction?**

While in deduction, the conclusion is entailed in the premises and its truth is guaranteed by the truth of the premises, induction is the reasoning process in which the conclusion is supposed to follow from the premises with a degree of probability rather than absolute certainty. In other words, in inductive reasoning, the premises provide support for the conclusion, but they cannot supply full assurance of its truth. Inductive conclusions are tentative and subject to revision with the emergence of further evidence. Therefore, if the premises in inductive reasoning are presumed to be true, it is still likely for the conclusion to be false.

E.g. 1 *Premise: The first bus has always arrived at my station at 6:05 for the last five days.*
  Conclusion: The first bus arrives at my station at 6:05.

E.g. 2 *Premise: Fifteen of your twenty classmates order the same dish at lunch.*
  Conclusion: Therefore, that dish probably tastes good.

Even if the premises are true in the arguments, it allows for the conclusions to be false.

■ **Common Types of Inductive Reasoning**

Unlike deduction which can be represented by its classic form of syllogism, induction does not have a single, standard structure. Typically, inductive reasoning involves moving from specific instances to broad generalizations, but that cannot cover all cases. There are many types of inductive reasoning that people regularly employ, both formally and informally. The following are some of the most common types.

Type	Example
Inductive generalization: Such reasoning relies on characteristics of a sample population to conclude about the population as a whole.	Premise: All the swans I have seen are white. Conclusion: All swans are white.
Statistical syllogism: It argues from premises regarding a portion of a population to a conclusion about a particular member or certain part of that population.	Premise: 90% of the swans my sister has seen are white. Ruby is a swan she has seen on one of her global travels. Conclusion: Ruby is a white swan.

Unit 2 Classical Patterns of Arguments: Induction

(continued)

Type	Example
Analogical reasoning: In this type of reasoning, premises about shared properties between two or more groups are set to conclude about further shared property between them.	Premise: Swans look like geese and geese lay eggs. Conclusion: Swans also lay eggs.
Causal reasoning: It makes cause-and-effect connections between the premise and the conclusion.	Premise: There have always been swans on the lake in summer. Conclusion: The start of summer brings swans onto the lake.
Predictive reasoning: In this type, a conclusion about the future is drawn from a past sample.	Premise: There have always been swans on the lake in past summers. Conclusion: There will be swans this summer.

> **?**
>
> **What type of inductive argument is the following example?**
>
> A recent experiment revealed that people who completed a 7-day strict GM diet plan were found to be healthier on average than the people who discontinued the diet halfway and returned to their old food habits. Clearly, the diet plan is at least partly responsible for making people healthy.

■ **Evaluation of Inductive Arguments**

Whereas deductive arguments can be pinned down to sound or unsound ones, inductive arguments lie on a spectrum that ranges from very **weak** to very **strong**, based on the quantity and quality of the premises and the extent to which they support the conclusion. An inductive argument is considered strong when its premises provide compelling evidence that renders its conclusion more likely true than false, and it is weak when its premises cannot provide such evidence.

> **?**
>
> **Which one of the two examples is stronger? Why?**
>
> *Example 1*
> **Premise:** Prices on the four items I bought in the campus store are higher than the same items in the downtown supermarket.
> **Conclusion:** The campus store is a more expensive place to shop.
>
> *Example 2*
> **Premise:** Prices on the twenty items I bought in the campus store are higher than the same items in the downtown supermarket.
> **Conclusion:** The campus store is probably a more expensive place to shop.

Extensive Reading 4

While we can decide on the validity of a deductive argument for certain, the evaluation of inductive reasoning is inherently a matter of probability as it is often based on sample data that can shift the strength of the argument with further evidence. That makes the assessment of inductive arguments more complex than that of deductive ones. However, despite the varied types, inductive arguments can generally be assessed from the following aspects of premises:

❖ Size of the data

—Is the sample big enough? Is the evidence sufficiently extensive?

In some cases, it is possible to observe all the instances in a particular situation. For example, by examining the prices of all items available in both stores on campus and in town, we can arrive at accurate and precise conclusions about the prices in the two stores. However, in most cases, our ability to make definitive observations about everything is limited. In this sense, a sufficiently large sample size or extensive evidence will increase the likelihood of the conclusion being true rather than false.

❖ Quality of the data

—Is the sample unbiased and representative? Is the evidence relevant and conclusive?

Even a large sample can hardly yield a reliable conclusion if it is not representative and unbiased. For example, a study on women's attitudes toward marriage should not be based solely on a sample of female college students, no matter how large the size of the sample is, as it excludes women of different age groups, educational backgrounds, marital status, etc.

What is your evaluation of the example argument here? Is it strong? Why or why not?
Both eagles and chickens are birds, both have feathers, and both lay eggs. So, since there is nothing wrong with eating chickens, there must be nothing wrong with eating eagles.

Generally, there is no sharp line between strong and weak. For example:

Every time I've walked by that dog, it hasn't tried to bite me. So, the next time I walk by that dog it won't try to bite me.

The argument would be stronger the more times "I" did walk by the dog safely, and be weaker the fewer times "I" have walked by the dog.

Despite their differences, inductive reasoning and deductive reasoning often go together and complement each other in our daily lives and studies. As both of them are crucial and beneficial to us all, professionally and personally, integrating induction and deduction is essential for us, especially in becoming effective arguers and critical readers.

Unit 2 Classical Patterns of Arguments: Induction

 Enhancing Your Critical Reading

Activity 1 Distinguish and Evaluate Inductive Arguments

Decide on what type of inductive reasoning each of the following statements belongs to. Determine whether they are strong or weak, and give your reasons.

Statement	Type	Strong or Weak	Reason
1. All of Jefferson's previous 10 novels have been popular. Therefore, his next novel will probably be popular, too.			
2. Based on a survey of the juniors at our university, approximately thirty-two percent expect to go abroad for further study after graduation. Lucas is a junior at our university. So, chances are that Lucas is planning to go abroad for further study after graduation.			
3. We should not blame the media for deteriorating moral standards. Social media are like weather reporters who report the facts. We do not blame weather reports for telling us that the weather is bad.			
4. All the children in this daycare center like to play with Lego. All children must like to play with Lego.			
5. Every time we have a full moon, people behave strangely. So, the full moon must have caused the strange behavior.			

Activity 2 Compare and Summarize

Compare deduction and induction, summarize their characteristics and fill in the blanks.

Deduction	Induction
If the premises are true, the conclusion has to be true.	
It reasons from the general principles to some specific facts.	
	It can be regarded as a "bottom-up approach" in which one starts from an observation, detects patterns, formulates a hypothesis, and reaches a conclusion or theory.

Extensive Reading 4

(continued)

Deduction	Induction
A sound deductive argument depends on its validity and the truth of the premises.	

Text A: How Art Movements Tried to Make Sense of the World in the Wake of the 1918 Flu Pandemic

Preparatory Work

(Source: https://www.healingmagazine.org/the-healing-power-of-art/)

Do you love art? How important is art to our life?

Which branch of art do you love most? Why? Recommend to your group or your class one or two of your favorite works in that branch. Which works of art from your classmates attract you most?

The Importance of Art in Life

My Favorite Works of Art

The Most Appealing Works of Art from My Classmates

(continued)

📖 Reading the Text

> The 1918 flu pandemic, together with the sense of trauma and despair, isolation and emptiness after or even before the pandemic, has left its imprint deep on the world of Western fine art.

How Art Movements Tried to Make Sense of the World in the Wake of the 1918 Flu Pandemic

Anna Purna Kambhampaty[1]

1 On Feb. 7, 1918, the artist Egon Schiele[2], then 27, once again looked to his mentor, Gustav Klimt[3], to be his muse. But this time, Schiele had to visit the morgue of Allgemeines Krankenhaus, the Vienna General Hospital, to make his drawings of the renowned painter. The day before, Klimt had died of a stroke that many historians believe was a result of the flu. Schiele's visit resulted in three haunting drawings of a deceased Klimt's head, showing his face deformed from the stroke.

2 That same year, Schiele began working on a painting, *The Family*, which was meant to be a portrait of himself, his wife and their future child. But before he could finish the piece, his wife, who was six months pregnant, died of the flu. Three days later, Schiele's life was also taken by the flu.

3 Norwegian painter Edvard Munch[4] also found inspiration in the disease. The artist made *Self-Portrait With the Spanish Flu* and *Self-Portrait After the Spanish Flu*, detailing his own experience contracting and surviving the illness. These paintings, characterized by Munch's obsession with existential drama, speak to feelings of trauma and despair that were widespread amid a pandemic that killed at least 50 million people. "Illness, insanity, and death… kept watch over my cradle," the artist once said, "and accompanied me all my life."

Edvard Munch's "Self-Portrait with the Spanish Flu", 1919 (Nasjonalmuseet)

4 It could be easy to think that these works are the only famous examples of the impact of the 1918 flu on the world of Western fine art. Though the ongoing fight against COVID-19 has drawn renewed attention to the pandemic of about a century ago, the influenza pandemic has long been largely overshadowed by World War I—

in public memory as well as contemporary thought—even though the flu had a higher death toll. In light of wartime efforts, news about the initial spread of the 1918 flu was played down in many places. "Do not worry too much about the disease," wrote the *Times of India*, in a country where 6% of the population ended up dying from the illness. In addition, many artists were sent to war during this time or died prematurely of the flu themselves.

5   But the flu did not go unnoticed by artists. Rather, the outbreak magnified the absurdity of the moment, according to art historian Corinna Kirsch. For many, World War I and the flu combined with political upheavals (such as the collapse of the Ottoman Empire and the rise of newly-formed communist governments) and social issues (such as gender and income inequality) to create a perception of the universe as chaotic and hopeless. A sense of meaninglessness spread, and people started to lose faith in their governments, existing social structures and accepted moral values. Everyday life felt ridiculous. The art movements that came out of this period explored this hopelessness, tried to fight against it and showed the ways in which everyone was trying to cope.

6   The Dada movement[5] in particular seized on this absurdity as inspiration. The Dadaists wanted to create a new form of art, one that could replace previous notions altogether. Collage became a popular medium at the time; "many artists were dealing with the modern era and the horrors of war through strategies of cutting, reassembling and remixing," explains Kirsch. One 1922 piece by Hannah Höch[6], the only woman who was part of the Berlin Dada group, parodied a traditional German guest book by collecting Dada sayings rather than the typical well-wishes from house guests. One saying included in the piece was from the poet Richard Hülsenbeck: "Death is a thoroughly Dadaist affair."

7   George Grosz[7], another Dada artist, painted *The Funeral* around 1918, depicting distorted human figures haphazardly overlapping one another in what appears to be a never-ending street, surrounded by nightclubs and buildings. In the middle of the crowd is a skeleton perched on top of a coffin drinking from a bottle. "In a strange street by night, a hellish procession of dehumanized figures mills, their faces reflecting alcohol, syphilis, plague… I painted this protest against a humanity that had gone insane," Grosz later said of his hellscape.

8   Though Dadaism was mostly nihilistic in its approach, "there was also a utopian impulse at work with many artists who wanted to create an entirely new world and revolution," says Kirsch.

9   With this impulse in mind, architect Walter Gropius[8] founded the Bauhaus School in Weimar, Germany, in 1919. The Bauhaus aimed to bridge art and design, training students to reject frivolous ornamentation in order to create art objects that were practical and useful in everyday life. Marcel Breuer[9], who started at the Bauhaus in 1920 and eventually taught there, designed furnishings that historians believe were influenced by the flu. In contrast to the heavy, upholstered furniture that was popular at the time, Breuer's minimalist pieces

were made of hygienic wood and tubular steel, able to facilitate cleaning. Lightweight and movable, works like the designer's bicycle-inspired Wassily Chair and Long Chair met modern sanitary needs by being easy to disinfect and rid of dust build-up.

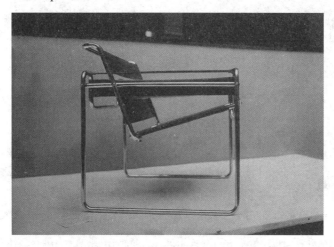

Wassily Chair, B3, design by Marcel Breuer at Bauhaus School (Gamma-Keystone/Getty Images)

10   "The rise of modern architecture and design in the 1920s was inextricably linked to the prevailing discourse on health and social hygiene," says Monica Obniski, curator of decorative arts and design at Atlanta's High Museum of Art.

11   To other artists dealing with the horrors of the time, abstraction was a way to escape reality. "Abstraction became a defining sense of that moment in time. There was a definite relationship [between] non-objective, non-realistic art and the horrors of what was going in the world," says Jeff Rosenheim, Curator in Charge of The Metropolitan Museum of Art's Department of Photographs. This was seen in many paintings and photographs made during the time. [*View of Rooftops*], a 1917 photograph of a desolate New York City scene, made by Morton Schamberg[10], is one example of this. The photograph, shot at an oblique angle, abstracts the cityscape in a Cubist manner and lacks any signs of human life. Schamberg died of the flu in 1918.

12   Further, in 1917, *Fountain* was unveiled under the pseudonym R. Mutt. The work consisted of a standard urinal, signed and dated, and thrust the art world into discussions of what was and wasn't to be considered art for years to come. It is widely believed that "R. Mutt" was Marcel Duchamp[11], but the subject has been up for debate. Art historian Michael Lobel argues that R. Mutt could also have been Schamberg. We aren't able to know for sure because of the artist's premature death from the flu. "Schamberg's relatively early death not only cut short his career but also means that we have little to no recorded testimony from him on these and related matters. In his case, then, the pandemic registers mostly as a telltale absence in our account of the period," Lobel has written in *Art Forum*.

Marcel Duchamp: *Fountain* (Source: https://www.britannica.com/art/Dada)

[13] Just as the 1918 flu pandemic was an inescapable part of the zeitgeist of the time, the coronavirus pandemic has already become so today. Though we might not know exactly how COVID-19 will affect art and art movements to come, the visual culture has already shifted.

[14] "Photographers discovering empty streets and how our cities look without people show a kind of sad beauty to these urban metropolises around the world," says Rosenheim. The empty cityscapes being captured and shared "aren't depicting the pandemic, but the effects of isolation and emptiness, psychologically." Others have argued that, as a result of the quarantine, nude selfies have become high art.

[15] As was the case in 1918, the pandemic is just one part of a larger mood that predated the disease. Isolation, stillness and the impacts of consumerism were already themes being explored through art in recent decades. For example, Andreas Gursky's[12] 1996 photograph *Prada II* shows a display case that is completely void of product and lit with sterile, fluorescent lights—an image that now calls to mind news photos of store shelves left empty amid the pandemic. Gregory Crewdson's[13] early 2000s "Beneath the Roses" series captures with a surreal ghostliness the desolate corners of small towns, evoking the urban loneliness of Edward Hopper's[14] paintings, which are being disseminated widely on social media today.

Andreas Gursky's "Prada II", 1996 (Courtesy the artist/Gagosian/The Metropolitan Museum of Art)

¹⁶ These works were created before the novel coronavirus swept the world, but they speak to the current moment—proving that, as was the case in the past, Rosenheim says, "we don't need a pandemic to create chaotic, psychologically traumatic imagery."

(Source: This article was published on *Time* on May 5, 2020.)

Notes

1. **Anna Purna Kambhampaty** is a writer covering gender, race, and culture.
2. **Egon Schiele** (1890-1918) was an Austrian Expressionist painter and a major figurative painter of the early 20th century.
3. **Gustav Klimt** (1862-1918) was an Austrian symbolist painter and a founding member of the school of painting known as the Vienna Secession.
4. **Edvard Munch** (1863-1944) was a Norwegian painter and printmaker whose 1893 painting *The Scream*, or *The Cry*, has become one of Western art's most acclaimed images.
5. **Dada** was an artistic and literary movement of the early 20th century in Europe and the United States as a reaction to the horrors and folly of World War I. Dadaism mocked and antagonized the conventions of art itself, emphasizing the illogical, irrational, and absurd.
6. **Hannah Höch** (1889-1978) was a German Dada artist, most recognized for her pioneering photomontage compositions that explore Weimar-era perceptions of gender and ethnic differences.
7. **George Grosz** (1893-1959) was a German artist known especially for his caricatures and paintings of Berlin life in the 1920s.
8. **Walter Gropius** (1883-1969) was a German American architect, educator, and founder of the Bauhaus School, a revolutionary art school in Germany. Gropius is widely regarded as one of the pioneering masters of modernist architecture.
9. **Marcel Breuer** (1902-1981) was a Hungarian-American architect and furniture designer, one of the most influential exponents of the International Style. Best known for his iconic chair designs, Breuer was concerned with attaining the Bauhaus objective of integrating art and industry.
10. **Morton Schamberg** (1881-1918) was an American modernist painter and photographer, a pioneer of the Precisionism art movement and one of the first American adopters of the Cubist style.
11. **Marcel Duchamp** (1887-1968) was a French-American painter and sculptor whose work is associated with Cubism and conceptual art. He challenged the very notion of what is art by breaking down the boundaries between works of art and everyday objects with his readymades.
12. **Andreas Gursky** (1955-) is a German photographer and professor at the Kunstakademie Düsseldorf, Germany. He is known for his large-format architecture and landscape color photographs, often employing a high point of view.
13. **Gregory Crewdson** (1962-) is an American photographer best known for staging large-scale, cinematic, psychologically charged scenes set in suburban landscapes and interiors.
14. **Edward Hopper** (1882-1967) was an American painter and printmaker whose realistic depictions of everyday urban scenes expose the isolation of the individual within the modern city.

Extensive Reading 4

Remembering and Understanding

Activity 1 Information Collection

Though this text does not introduce the 1918 flu pandemic fully, it has given some information about it. Write a brief introduction to that pandemic based on the information from the text.

Activity 2 Match Pictures and Their Captions

Match the following pictures and their captions. What message can you read from each picture?

	Match Pictures and Captions	My Interpretation of Each Picture
Picture 1	A. Edvard Munch's "Self-Portrait after the Spanish Flu", 1919	
Picture 2	B. Egon Schiele's "Gustav Klimt on his death bed", 1918	
Picture 3	C. Morton Schamberg's "View of Rooftops", 1917	
Picture 4	D. George Grosz's "The Funeral", 1918	

1.
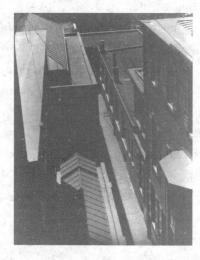

2.

Unit 2 Classical Patterns of Arguments: Induction

3.    4.

Activity 3 Multiple-choice Questions

Choose the best answer(s) from the choices given based on the text.

1. Which of the following artists died of the flu in the 1918 flu pandemic? Choose all that apply.

    A. Egon Schiele   B. Gustav Klimt

    C. Edvard Munch   D. Hannah Höch

    E. George Grosz   F. Walter Gropius

    G. Marcel Breuer   H. Morton Schamberg

    I. Marcel Duchamp

2. Why did Egon Schiele go to Gustav Klimt on Feb. 7, 1918?

    A. He went to take care of Gustav since Gustav was ill.

    B. He went to attend Gustav's funeral.

    C. He wanted to get some inspiration from Gustav for his painting.

    D. He wanted to make drawings of the deceased renowned painter.

3. Which of the following feelings is not expressed in Edvard Munch's paintings about the flu?

    A. Trauma.   B. Hopelessness.   C. Striving.   D. Despair.

4. Why has the 1918 flu pandemic long been neglected by people?

    A. Because it was overshadowed by World War I.

    B. Because it had a higher death toll than World War I.

    C. Because the initial spread of the pandemic was not serious.

    D. Because it was prevalent only in India.

5. How would many people feel in the period after the outbreak of the 1918 flu pandemic? Choose all that apply.

Extensive Reading 4

    A. Absurd.   B. Chaotic.   C. Hopeless.   D. Meaningless.   E. Horrified.

6. Which of the following statements describes the Dada movement appropriately?

    A. It was more popular among women painters than their male counterparts.

    B. It was inspired by the sense of absurdity around the time of the flu pandemic.

    C. It relied more on utopian impulse than on a nihilistic approach.

    D. It created a new form of art—collage.

7. What are the features of the photograph [*View of Rooftops*]? Choose all that apply.

    A. Its slanting angle.

    B. Its Cubist manner.

    C. The disappearance of signs of human life.

    D. The death of its creator in the flu pandemic.

8. According to the article, what is special about the work *Fountain* in Para. 12? Choose all that apply.

    A. It is a work of abstraction.

    B. Its creator is not ascertained.

    C. It aroused discussions on the scope of art in the following years.

    D. It was unveiled before the flu pandemic.

Reasoning and Analyzing

Answer the following questions.

1. The article explains the neglect of the 1918 flu pandemic at that time. What do you think the author's attitude on this neglect is?

2. What does the author imply by saying that the outbreak "magnified" the absurdity of the moment in Para. 5?

3. In which way would George Grosz (Para. 7) and Marcel Breuer (Para. 9) be different in their artistic expression?

4. What does "abstraction" mean as a way to escape reality?

5. According to Michael Lobel in Para. 12, what is the impact of Schamberg's death?

6. How has the visual culture shifted by COVID-19 according to the author?

7. What does the author intend to illustrate with examples of Andreas Gursky's and Gregory Crewdson's works in Para. 15?

8. According to the article, in which ways are the 1918 flu pandemic and the COVID-19 pandemic similar?

9. How does the author argue for the huge impact of the 1918 flu pandemic on the world of Western fine art? In an inductive way or a deductive way?

Reflecting and Creating

Topics for discussion and writing.

1. One major way for human beings to make progress is to learn from history. What can we learn from the 1918 flu pandemic? Collect more information on that pandemic and summarize some lessons from it. Then compare man's responses to the 1918 flu pandemic and the COVID-19 pandemic. What progress have man made?

2. The piece of work *Fountain* "thrust the art world into discussions of what was and wasn't to be considered art" (Para. 12). Do you think *Fountain* can be taken as art? What should or shouldn't be considered art in your view? Give your explanation.

3. In this world with increasingly advanced science and technology, do you think people need art more or less than before? Why? Organize your ideas and develop them into a paragraph of about 150 words with clarity and coherence.

Extensive Reading 4

Text B: Creative Thinking in Both Science and the Art Is Not for the Faint of Heart

Preparatory Work

Conventionally, science and art are regarded as two fundamentally different branches of study and people in these two fields are equally different from each other. Do you agree on the entire differences between science and art? What do you think their relationship should be? In which way are they similar to each other? In which way are they different? Collect some examples of their influence on each other.

(Source: https://www.duarte.com/presentation-lessons-from-scientists-who-dance/)

Relation Between Science and Art	
Their Similarities	
Their Differences	
Examples of Their Influence on Each Other	

Reading the Text

> Though arts and sciences employ different content, tools, and approaches to shape their message, they both hold creativity as the source of innovation and progress. But how are the fruits of creativity and the innovators behind them truly received in the real world? Are they always acclaimed and embraced?

Creative Thinking in Both Science and the Arts Is Not for the Faint of Heart

Avi Loeb[1]

Napoleon Sarony *Getty Images* (Source: https://www.scientificamerican.com/article/creative-thinking-in-both-science-and-the-arts-is-not-for-the-faint-of-heart/)

1   Over the past few months, I've been invited to speak with well-known writers, musicians and film producers regarding my recent book, *Extraterrestrial*. Prior to these conversations, I was on the receiving (and admiring) end of their artistic work, but now they were curious about my own research as a scientist. These exchanges led me to recognize the similarities between innovation in the arts and the sciences. In general, it appears that the craft of creating our most imaginative frontiers cannot be formulated as a cookbook recipe.

2   In sciences and arts alike, creativity appears magically as an unpredictable fountain of inspiration from the subconscious. Its unexpected content breaks routines within traditional thinking. It delivers something new that is distinct from common practices, often taking people out of their comfort zone because it is ahead of its time. As a result, many innovators are ridiculed and denied the recognition they deserve when they need it the most. When the Greek philosopher Socrates questioned people in public through dialogues and failed to acknowledge the gods that the democratic city-state of Athens worshipped, he was accused of corrupting the youth and was executed by being forced to drink poison. Today, Socrates would have been canceled on Athenian social media. As Oscar Wilde[2] said: "A writer is someone who has taught [the] mind to misbehave."

3   There are many examples of such circumstances. The revolutionary theory of continental drift advanced by Alfred Wegener in 1912, was rejected by mainstream geologists for four decades and only became popular after the mechanism of plate tectonics was recognized. In 1933 Fritz Zwicky inferred the existence of large quantities of invisible mass in the Coma galaxy cluster, which he labeled "dark matter", but it took four decades for this notion to gain traction within the astronomy community. The doctoral thesis of Cecilia Payne-Gaposchkin at Radcliffe-Harvard concluded in 1925 that the surface of the sun is made mostly of hydrogen, but this idea was dismissed by Henry Norris Russell, the prominent director of the Princeton University Observatory. Four years later he realized that she was right. In the 1962 book *Astronomy of the 20th Century*, Otto Struve and Velta Zebergs described Payne-Gaposchkin's work as "undoubtedly the most brilliant Ph.D. thesis ever written in astronomy".

4   Following his own compass on another frontier, Otto Struve suggested that we search for hot Jupiters[3] around other stars in 1952, four long decades before the 1995 discovery of 51 Pegasi b[4] by Didier Queloz and Michel Mayor—which earned them the 2019 Nobel Prize in Physics. In biology, the rules of genetic heredity formulated by Gregor Mendel in 1866 were ignored by the scientific community, rediscovered by Hugo de Vries and Carl Correns three decades later, and eventually explained by the molecular chemistry of DNA almost a century after Mendel's work.

5   The same fate applies to innovative artists. Vincent van Gogh[5] was considered a madman and a failure throughout his life, but his reputation changed to that of a misunderstood genius when elements of his painting style were incorporated by expressionists several decades after his suicide in 1890. Today, van Gogh's paintings are among the most expensive ever sold. The writer Samuel Beckett[6] did not get his first novel published, and so he shelved it. The novel was eventually published in 1992, three years after Beckett's death, and 23 years after he was awarded the 1969 Nobel Prize in Literature. Quoting Wilde: "An idea that is not dangerous is unworthy of being called an idea at all."

(Image: Shutterstock.com; retrieved from: https://www.forbesindia.com/blog/technology/the-art-and-science-of-digital/)

6 Life offers two ways of acquiring commodities. One is by collecting existing items, and the other is by creating things that never existed before. Whereas most items on the shelves of supermarkets are mass-produced, entities that are newly created by artists or scientists are initially unique.

7 Just like aging wine, a product of creative work acquires quality over time. It is colored by the response of the audience as well as by imitations. The initial circumstances are reminiscent of an admirable infant. It is fascinating for a scientist or an artist to watch the interaction of their creation with the world, just as it is for parents to watch their children.

8 Arts and sciences have different content and hence adopt different tools to shape their message. They constitute complementary ways of viewing reality which are not a substitute for each other. Scientific innovation translates to new technological devices, like global positioning systems for navigation based on Albert Einstein's general theory of relativity. Artistic innovation translates to new cultural assets, like Pablo Picasso's[7] Cubism[8]—which sparked related movements in music, literature and architecture. The products of the creative process are surprising at first in all venues of human inventiveness.

9 But what counts as ingenuity at first sight, could in retrospect be considered as inevitable. In the physical sciences, one could argue that reality exists before it is discovered. The same could be said about the arts. As Michelangelo[9] noted when asked how he produced beautiful sculptures from a block of marble: "The sculpture is already complete within the marble block, before I start my work. It is already there, I just have to chisel away the superfluous material."

10 Both arts and sciences advance through open-minded iterations. The alternative of staying within traditional boundaries suppresses the exploration of new territories. As Oscar Wilde said: "Consistency is the last refuge of the unimaginative."

11 Recognizing the crucial role that imagination plays in advancing both arts and sciences would translate to a culture that fosters innovation by rewarding creativity. Conventional groupthink could be circumvented by populating selection committees of funding agencies with creative individuals rather than with traditional thinkers. A culture of innovation would also benefit from overlap spaces where scientists and artists interact. In deriving his theory of gravity Albert Einstein[10] was inspired by the philosopher Ernst Mach[11], and Einstein's new notions of space and time inspired Picasso's paintings.

12 Creativity in arts and sciences establishes a backdrop for human existence, as the content it invents gives pleasure and meaning to our lives. The human act of creation is an infinite-sum game, from which all of us benefit. And we can all participate in the creative process, as long as we follow another famous piece of wisdom: "Be yourself; everyone else is already taken."

(Source: The article was published on *scientificamerican.com* on June 3, 2021.)

Extensive Reading 4

> **Notes**
>
> 1. **Avi Loeb** is former chair (2011-2020) of the astronomy department at Harvard University, founding director of Harvard's Black Hole Initiative and director of the Institute for Theory and Computation at the Harvard-Smithsonian Center for Astrophysics. He also chairs the Board on Physics and Astronomy of the National Academies and the advisory board for the Breakthrough Starshot project, and is a member of President's Council of Advisors on Science and Technology. Loeb is the author of *Extraterrestrial: The First Sign of Intelligent Life Beyond Earth* (Houghton Mifflin Harcourt).
> 2. **Oscar Wilde** (1854-1900) was an Irish poet and dramatist, best remembered for his acclaimed works including the Gothic novel *The Picture of Dorian Gray* (1891) and the stage satire *The Importance of Being Earnest* (1895), as well as his oft-quoted witticisms, flamboyant style and infamous imprisonment (1895-1897) for homosexuality.
> 3. **Hot Jupiters** are gas giant planets, thought to be akin to Jupiter and Saturn, that orbit their parent stars with typical orbital periods of only a few days.
> 4. **51 Pegasi b** is a gas giant exoplanet that orbits a G-type star. Its discovery was announced in 1995.
> 5. **Vincent van Gogh** (1853-1890) was a Dutch painter, one of the world's greatest artists with paintings such as "Starry Night" and "Sunflowers". The striking colour, emphatic brushwork, and contoured forms of his work highly influenced the current of Expressionism in modern art. Though widely popular nowadays, Vincent van Gogh remained poor and virtually unknown throughout his life and suffered from mental illness.
> 6. **Samuel Beckett** (1906-1989) was an Irish novelist, playwright, critic and poet, winner of the Nobel Prize for Literature in 1969, best known for his plays, especially *Waiting for Godot* (1952).
> 7. **Pablo Picasso** (1881-1973) was a Spanish painter, sculptor, printmaker, ceramicist, and stage designer. Considered one of the greatest and most influential artists of the 20th century, Picasso is most famous for paintings like "Guernica" and the creation of Cubism with Georges Braque.
> 8. **Cubism** was a highly influential visual arts style of the 20th century, created principally by the artists Pablo Picasso and Georges Braque in Paris between 1907 and 1914, which employs geometric shapes in depictions of humans and other forms.
> 9. **Michelangelo** (1475-1564) was an Italian Renaissance sculptor, painter, architect, and poet, universally accepted as one of the greatest artists in the history of art. Michelangelo's most seminal works include the "David" and "Pieta" sculptures and the Sistine Chapel and "Last Judgment" paintings.
> 10. **Albert Einstein** (1879-1955) was a German-born physicist, generally considered the most influential physicist of the 20th century. He developed the special and general theories of relativity and won the Nobel Prize for Physics in 1921 for his explanation of the phenomenon known as the photoelectric effect.
> 11. **Ernst Mach** (1838-1916) was an Austrian physicist and philosopher who established important principles of optics, mechanics, and wave dynamics, and is considered a founder of the philosophy of science.

Remembering and Understanding

Answer the following questions.

1. What did the exchanges with writers, musicians and film producers allow the author to realize?

2. How would Socrates have been received today?

3. What does the author refer to by "such circumstances" in Para. 3 and "the same fate" in Para. 5 respectively?

4. What is like aging wine? In which way are they alike? What is compared to an admirable infant? In which way are they similar?

5. Why does the author refer to global positioning systems for navigation and Pablo Picasso's Cubism?

6. How could ingenious works in sciences and arts be inevitable?

7. What does the author mean by "open-minded iterations" in Para. 10? What result does "the alternative of staying within traditional boundaries" (Para. 10) lead to?

8. What measures does the author propose to build innovation and cultivate creativity?

Extensive Reading 4

Reasoning and Analyzing

Activity 1 Answer the Following Questions

1. What does the author imply about a cookbook recipe? What is the difference between making a cookbook recipe and creating works in sciences and arts?

2. What is the author's attitude toward innovators?

3. What conclusion would the examples listed in Para. 3, 4, 5 reach? Which pattern of reasoning does the author take to reach this conclusion?

4. What does the sentence "The products of the creative process are surprising at first in all venues of human inventiveness" (Para. 8) imply? How does it relate to the next paragraph?

5. What kind of game is an "infinite-sum game" (Para. 12)? Why does the author regard the human act of creation as an infinite-sum game?

6. In which ways are sciences and arts similar to and different from each other according to the text?

Activity 2 Implications of Quotes

In the text, the author presents many quotes, especially from Oscar Wilde. Why does the author give each quote? What are the implications of these quotes as used in the text? Give your understanding of their implications in the following table.

Quotes	Implications in Text
"A writer is someone who has taught [the] mind to misbehave." (Para. 2)	

(continued)

Quotes	Implications in Text
"An idea that is not dangerous is unworthy of being called an idea at all." (Para. 5)	
"Consistency is the last refuge of the unimaginative." (Para. 10)	
"Be yourself; everyone else is already taken." (Para. 12)	

 Reflecting and Creating

Topics for discussion and writing.

1. In this article, the author has listed many similarities and differences between sciences and arts. Do you agree with the author on his list? What other similarities and differences can you locate?

2. The author claims in the article that in sciences and arts alike, "what counts as ingenuity at first sight, could in retrospect be considered as inevitable."(Para. 9) What does the author mean by this proposal? Since ingenious works come inevitably, what is the significance of man's work then?

3. The author quotes many times from Oscar Wilde throughout the text. Of so many writers, artists, and scientists, why do you think the author picks out Oscar Wilde and quotes from him? Collect some information about Oscar Wilde and his achievements, and try to make out the reasons for the author's choice. Develop your ideas into a paragraph. Remember to organize your ideas and justify your reasons.

Summary

 Self-reflection

Fill out the checklist.

Area	Yes/No?	Notes/Comment
I know what induction is.		
I know some typical types of inductive arguments.		

Extensive Reading 4

(continued)

Area	Yes/No?	Notes/Comment
I know how to tell the cogency of inductive reasoning.		
I know how to evaluate inductive arguments.		
I know more about how fine art reflects reality and emotions.		
I have a deeper understanding of the importance and influence of creativity in science and art.		
I know more about the relationship between science and art.		

 Value Cultivation

Activity 1 Group the Quotes

Read the following quotes. What is the key message in each statement? Group those who would most likely agree with each other. Please note that there may be more than one group.

1. Every great advance in science has issued from a new audacity of imagination.　　　—John Dewey
2. If you hear a voice within you say "you cannot paint," then by all means paint, and that voice will be silenced.　　　—Vincent Van Gogh
3. Without art, the crudeness of reality would make the world unbearable.　　　—George Bernard Shaw
4. Without tradition, art is a flock of sheep without a shepherd. Without innovation, it is a corpse.
　　　—Winston Churchill
5. Science is not only a disciple of reason but, also, one of romance and passion.　　　—Stephen Hawking
6. 艺术为人类精神之食粮，即人类精神之营养品。音乐为养耳，绘画为养目，美味为养口。养耳、养目、养口，为养身心也。如有损于身心，是鸦片鸩酒，非艺术也。——潘天寿《听天阁画谈随笔》
7. 艺术是最高的养生方法，不但足以养我中华民族，且能养成全人类的福祉寿考也。
——黄宾虹《养生之道》
8. 艺术和科学的共同基础是人类的创造力，它们追求的目标都是真理的普遍性，事实上是一个硬币的两面。　　　——李政道《科学和艺术——在炎黄艺术馆的讲话》
9. 文艺反映社会，不是通过概念对社会进行抽象，而是通过文字、颜色、声音、情感、情节、画面、图像等进行艺术再现。因此，社会的色彩有多么斑斓，文艺作品的色彩就应该有多么斑斓；社会的情境有多么丰富，文艺作品的情境就应该有多么丰富；社会的韵味有多么淳厚，文艺作品的韵味就应该有多么淳厚。
——习近平 2016 年 11 月 30 日在中国文联十大、中国作协九大开幕式上的讲话
10. 创新贵在独辟蹊径、不拘一格，但一味标新立异、追求怪诞，不可能成为上品，而很可能流于下品。要克服浮躁这个顽疾，抵制急功近利、粗制滥造，用专注的态度、敬业的精神、踏实的努力创作出更多高质量、高品位的作品。
——习近平 2016 年 11 月 30 日在中国文联十大、中国作协九大开幕式上的讲话

Unit 2 Classical Patterns of Arguments: Induction

Activity 2 Art and Science

The following two pieces of material express the features of art respectively. What is the message about art carried in each material? How different are they? What is your understanding of art in this respect?

1. Art is I; science is we.　　　　　　　　　　　　　　　　　　　　　　　—Claude Bernard

2. 人民的需要是文艺存在的根本价值所在。能不能搞出优秀作品，最根本的决定于是否能为人民抒写、为人民抒情、为人民抒怀。……

　　文艺只有植根现实生活、紧跟时代潮流，才能发展繁荣；只有顺应人民意愿、反映人民关切，才能充满活力。……

　　文艺的一切创新，归根到底都直接或间接来源于人民。"世事洞明皆学问，人情练达即文章。"艺术可以放飞想象的翅膀，但一定要脚踩坚实的大地。文艺创作方法有一百条、一千条，但最根本、最关键、最牢靠的办法是扎根人民、扎根生活。

　　　　　　　　　　——习近平 在文艺工作座谈会上的讲话（2014 年 10 月 15 日）

Message in Quote 1	
Message in Quote 2	
My Understanding	

Further Reading

1. What Is Art? by Leo Tolstoy
2. 习近平 2016 年 11 月 30 日在中国文联十大、中国作协九大开幕式上的讲话
3. 《艺术与科学文丛·1》，陈履生，中国科学技术大学出版社，2022 年 11 月

Unit 3
Aristotelian Model of Argument

Mastering Critical Reading

To construct a compelling argument, logical reasoning alone, while essential, is often insufficient to persuade effectively. Human beings are not swayed merely by logic and tight reasoning. In the real world, it takes many factors to work together to render an argument truly effective and powerful. In this light, understanding the Aristotelian model of persuasion can enhance our ability to explore the effectiveness of other's arguments and, at the same time, to empower those of our own.

The Aristotelian model, or classical model, of argument is developed by the renowned Greek philosopher and rhetorician Aristotle. He identified three key rhetorical appeals in arguments in his *Rhetoric* in 350 BCE: logos, as he termed, which refers to logical appeal; pathos, which is emotional appeal; and ethos, the ethical appeal. The three elements, when working together effectively, can significantly enhance an argument's persuasive power.

(Source: https://www.britannica.com/biography/Aristotle)

■ **Ethos (Ethical Appeal)**

Ethos, as Aristotle defined it, is "persuasion through character". It relates to the characteristics of the speakers or the writers which establish their credibility and trustworthiness. It is the way the writers or the speakers present themselves to the audience, specifically how reputable and respectable they are morally in the eyes of the audience as well as how knowledgeable or wise they are about their arguments.

Ethos is crucial in laying the foundation for an argument's success, as it is the credibility of the source that often determines the audience's initial reception. Aristotle considered ethos to be the most important element in an arguer's ability to persuade the audience, from which the possible success of the argument begins. He attributed one's credibility to intelligence, character, and goodwill, a principle that remains applicable in modern days. An audience can assess an arguer's credibility by examining whether they are knowledgeable and well-informed about the subject; whether they are morally upright and dependable, as well as truthful and honest in the use of evidence; whether they are with good intentions and fair-minded in considering the interests and needs of others as well as their own. In specific arguments, the proper use of tone, word choice, and respect for opposing views can also contribute to a strong ethos.

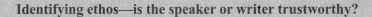

Identifying ethos—is the speaker or writer trustworthy?
✓ What are their credentials? Are they professional or authoritative in the field? Do they have the discussed experience themselves?
✓ Do they use reliable sources? Do they supply sufficient support? Have they done a substantial study on the topic? Do they give any sources of evidence?
✓ Are they fair-minded persons who have considered all sides of this issue? Do they include any counterarguments?

■ **Pathos (Emotional Appeal)**

Pathos targets the audience's emotions. Ideally, an audience can be convinced by the logic of an argument alone, but, as noted by Aristotle, people's reception of arguments can be influenced by their emotional state. By tapping into the audience's feelings, a speaker or writer can evoke an emotional response that aligns with their argument and thus increases the possibility of its reception. To employ pathos effectively, arguers need to be aware of their audience's feelings on the issue, their attitudes, values and beliefs that will affect their response to the argument. Pathos is often directed to evoke and amplify the latent feelings of the audience through various means, like story-telling, vivid imagery, and passionate language.

Appeal to the emotions of the audience is a legitimate and powerful way of persuasion, and if used properly, it can enhance persuasiveness prominently. However, as it can go unjustifiable or personal too easily, the audience must take a critical stance and keep healthy skepticism towards such persuasion through emotions. When reading emotional appeal, readers need to consider whether they are relevant to the argument or divert attention away from the issue under discussion, and whether they are used to assist the logical reasoning or for other purposes.

Identifying Pathos—Does the speaker or writer appeal to the emotions of the audience?
➤ Do they use loaded language or words that carry specific connotations, like commendatory or derogatory expressions in describing someone or some scene?
➤ Do they use individuals' stories to visualize the problem discussed? Do they give vivid descriptions when relating opinions or attitudes? What's the effect of these stories or descriptions?

■ **Logos (Logical Appeal)**

Logos is the appeal to logic and reason, focusing on the content of an argument. Aristotle maintained that the strength of an argument lies heavily on its logical coherence and the quality of the support provided. Establishing meaningful connections between evidence and claims, supporting claims with solid evidence, and even employing historical or literal analogies to create logical parallels are all elements of logos. For an argument to be taken seriously, the arguer must not only provide good evidence but also organize it appropriately. The audience needs to see how the evidence supports the point. While ethos and pathos involve

Extensive Reading 4

the human players of the arguer and the audience, logos is primarily concerned with the argument's inherent qualities.

Aristotle recognized two types of argumentation: induction and deduction. As we have learned, *induction* is primarily the process of reaching generalization from specifics, while *deduction* is the process of applying a generalization to a specific instance. Both are significant approaches for humans to know the world and ourselves.

What's more, good logic and clear reasoning are also helpful for an arguer to stand favorably to their audience as a sensible person, thus strengthening their ethos.

Identifying Logos—Does the speaker or writer appeal to the rational mind by using logic and evidence?
➢ Do they express their claims clearly and exactly?
➢ Do they include facts, statistics, or other kinds of evidence to support their points?
➢ Do they show the audience how ideas connect in a rational way?
➢ Do they commit any logical fallacy? Is there anything erroneous in their reasoning?

Enhancing Your Critical Reading

Activity 1 Rhetorical Triangle

Complete the following rhetorical triangle with the terms Logos, Pathos, Ethos and give a brief explanation to each of them.

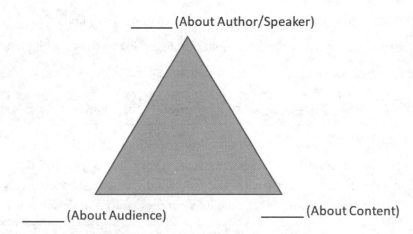

Term	Brief Explanation
Logos	
Ethos	
Pathos	

Activity 2 Identification of Appeals

Which appeal of ethos, pathos, and logos does each arguer intend to apply in the following excerpts respectively?

Excerpt 1 _____	Excerpt 2 _____
Others have marched with us down nameless streets of the South. They have languished in filthy, roach-infested jails, suffering the abuse and brutality of policemen who view them as "dirty nigger lovers". —Martin Luther King Jr., "Letter from Birmingham Jail"	Woz and I started Apple in my parents' garage when I was 20. We worked hard, and in 10 years Apple had grown from just the two of us in a garage into a $2 billion company with over 4000 employees. We had just released our finest creation—the Macintosh—a year earlier, and I had just turned 30... —Steve Jobs, Stanford Commencement Speech in 2005

Text A   Every Little Girl Wants to Be a Princess, Right?

Preparatory Work

Activity 1 Being a Princess/Prince

Have you ever dreamed of being a princess/prince when you were a kid? What kind of life would a princess/prince live in your imagination? What are the possible priorities and responsibilities of a princess/prince? Are there any disadvantages to being a princess/prince? Do you still dream of being a princess/prince now? Why or why not?

(Source: https://pluspng.com/png-crown-princess-9477.html)

Life of a Princess/Prince in My Dream	
Possible Priorities, Responsibilities, and Disadvantages	
My Dream of Being a Princess/Prince Now	

Extensive Reading 4

Activity 2 Who Is the Most Beautiful?

Do you like watching beauty pageants, competitions in which young women are judged for the most beautiful? How can women be judged in this respect since people's criteria of beauty vary greatly? Do you know any of the criteria for those pageants?

Like it or not, beauty pageants enjoy considerable popularity. What is your suggestion for the competition items and the criteria to judge contestants? Do you think this kind of competition is necessary at all?

Suggested Items in My Class	Suggested Criteria in My Class	Is It Necessary?

Reading the Text

> While little girls are aspiring to become beautiful and lovely princesses, competitions for the most beautiful and shining ones have gone astray. They exploit children and become harmful. It's time for adults to take the responsibility to protect not only the children but also the future of society.

Every Little Girl Wants to Be a Princess, Right?[1]
Mariah Jackson

(Source: https://wallpapercave.com/w/wp8950253)

[1] Beauty pageants have become a staple in American culture. Winners of pageants such as Miss America

are icons, representations of the ideal woman, and positive role models for young girls. So society says. More recently, however, a new type of pageant has increased in popularity to the point of being considered a national phenomenon. These pageants are just as glitzy, and the competition is just as fierce; the only difference is that these contestants are the miniature model. They are child beauty queens. The world of child beauty pageants has become a source of fascination, as well as contention, in our society. Networks such as TLC and WE TV have produced hit reality shows featuring the munchkin-sized divas because it sells, but one cannot help but wonder, how can parading children about on stage like show ponies be a positive thing? The truth is it is not. Beauty pageants are not a healthy activity for children because they force young girls to act like little adults, exhibit age-inappropriate sexuality, and have negative body image and mental health problems later in their lives. Children are the future of society, and even those who do not have children should be concerned about the direction of the culture they have to live in. Just because child beauty pageants *are* socially acceptable does not mean they should be. Our culture needs to eliminate child beauty pageants, at least in their current form.

2 While beauty pageants for kids have been around for a long time, their huge popularity is relatively recent. America's first televised child beauty pageant was held in 1960 in Miami, Florida, and it only aired on a local television station (Hilboldt-Stolley 2). Today, the "mini" beauty pageant industry is a multi-billion dollar-a-year endeavor (Giroux 31). Little girls compete in categories such as swimwear, beauty, talent, modeling, and glamour. They have spray tans, false eyelashes, flippers for their teeth, pounds of make-up, and dresses that cost hundreds of dollars each. Author Henry Giroux did extensive research on the child beauty pageant circuit for his article "Child Beauty Pageants and the Politics of Innocence". He then made this observation when describing the differences in the original beauty pageants and what we see now: "The children in the 1977 pageants wore little-girl dresses and ribbons in their hair; they embodied a child-like innocence in their appearance as they displayed their little girl talents—singing, tap dancing, and baton twirling. Not so with recent pageant shots." (43) That kind of simplicity does not exist in today's pageant world. Instead, it is a fierce competition for monetary prizes and the "grand supreme" title. This is the world we are putting our toddlers into while instructing them to "strut their stuff".

(Source: https://funguerilla.com/child-beauty-pageants-stolen-childhood/)

3 The hit television shows are another new aspect of the pageant life that has contributed to the explosion

of controversy. Shows like WE's *Little Miss Perfect* and TLC's *Toddlers and Tiaras* follow families in the child pageant circuit. Their cameras capture all the drama, makeovers, tantrums, and meltdowns that are a regular part of the important national pageants. TLC's network website describes the show: "Once at the pageant, it's all up to the judges and the drama ensues when every parent wants to prove that their child is beautiful." (TLC 2009) That quote alone is enough to shine a small light on the darker side of the glamorous exterior of pageants. The networks defend their shows, saying they are just documentaries of the life that thousands of children lead and that viewers must make their own judgments. Clearly, pushy parents are a part of the morbid attraction that those TV shows have for the masses, but with the video footage from these shows, it is hard to deny that these children are being exploited.

4   One way that pageants exploit children is in a sexual manner. The majority of participants are young enough that they should still be playing with baby dolls and jump ropes, yet they are performing routines that involve a lot of hip shaking and kissy faces. Combine those factors with the skimpy outfits, and many fittingly question how these pageant displays are any different than child pornography. Mark Davidson provides commentary in his 1997 article for *USA Today Magazine* entitled "Is the Media to Blame for Child Sex Victims"? He writes, "These pageants commercially flaunt kids' bodies, often converting preteen and preschool girls into sex puppets adorned with lipstick, mascara, false eyelashes, bleached hair, high heels, and satin-and-rhinestone gowns, and professionally coached in showgirl postures and movements." (1) Little girls like to play dress up, but there is no doubt that the way they are dressed for the competitions is catering to an adult preference. Sadly, their parents are the adults responsible for dressing these babies as Vegas showgirls and belly dancers. These children are not dressed to please a child's tastes; they are dressed to please adults, and adults have a sexualized view of what is beautiful.

5   Sexualizing children and preteens is wrong because it puts them at risk for more serious physical harm. The sexual aspect of pageants caters to a world bordering that of pedophiles and kiddy porn. Giroux argued that "the popular literature that supports the pageant culture fails to acknowledge that 'sexualized images of little girls may have dangerous implications in a world where 450,000 American children were reported as victims of sexual abuse in 1993'" (40). While pageants themselves are not sexual abuse, they can contribute to situations that result in the sexual abuse of children. Parents should be aware of this danger when they place their children in pageants. While parents are the ultimate decision makers for their minor children, there should be a line where society says "enough".

6   The famous case of JonBenet Ramsey's murder played a big role in bringing out the sexual aspect of the child beauty queen controversies. The six-year old pageant royalty was found dead in her basement on December 26, 1996. She had been sexually assaulted and then strangled and bludgeoned to death. The media went wild. Henry Giroux also studied the JonBenet case for his article, and he described the media attention

like this: "Major media networks, newspapers, and tabloids besieged the public with photographs and television footage of JonBenet, dubbed as the slain beauty queen, posing coquettishly in a tight dress, wearing bright red lipstick, her hair bleached blonde." (35) Many began to wonder whether or not her participation in beauty pageants had contributed to her untimely death, but no one knew who had killed her. Regardless, people were spooked, and beauty pageant entries dropped dramatically for a period of time. Although the facts of who killed her and why remain inconclusive to this day, the fact of the matter is, JonBenet was a young child forced to live an adult lifestyle. Her tragic death made the sexual aspect of pageants a point of national concern.

(Source: documentary *The Case of JonBenet Ramsey*)

7   Child beauty pageants are also harmful to the participants' self-esteem and mental health later on in life. The University of Minnesota conducted a study in 2005 on the relationship between beauty pageant participation as children and eating disorders and poor body image. While a relationship between pageants and eating disorders could not be nailed down, poor self-esteem and negative body image were apparent. Those two things are known to be symptoms of eating disorders, so a correlation between pageants and eating disorders does exist in an indirect way. The results stated, "Women who participated in childhood beauty pageants scored significantly higher on measures of body dissatisfaction, interpersonal distrust, and impulse dysregulation, than women who did not…" (Wonderlich et al. 297). Essentially, the women who were mini beauty queens grew up to hate their bodies, missed out on meaningful relationships, and struggled with self-control. Pageants teach young girls that they are only beautiful when they have unnatural amounts of makeup on. It also teaches them that they need to compare themselves to other girls, and if they do not compare favorably then they have failed. It teaches them to expect perfection of themselves, but perfection does not exist in our world. Therefore, pageants are setting them up to fail in their own minds and in their future social endeavors.

8   With all these apparent consequences of placing children in pageants, one has to ask oneself, "*what* are their parents thinking?" Pageant parents and other advocates of child pageants argue that these pageants are

way for their children to get ahead in life. They say that pageants are a great way for their children to pursue modeling careers or win money for college (Giroux 41). Reporter Lise Hilboldt-Stolley wrote an article entitled "Pretty Babies" from the viewpoint of a pageant mom. She shared the pro-pageant views of one of the pageant grandmothers with this statement, "they have good manners, high self-esteem, and they know how to act in public. You can go into a restaurant and see a table of pageant kids eating quietly, surrounded by rowdy, badly behaved kids all over the place"(3). But even with these supposed benefits, one has got to continue wondering if it is worth all the harm. It is possible to obtain these benefits from other activities or with different kinds of competitions. Young children, boys and girls, should be able to compete in activities that involve talent and educational leadership. These activities would help reap the benefits pageant parents say they see. The difference is that moving away from the make-up and adult clothing would encourage children to be children and cut down on the negative side effects of pageants as they currently exist.

[9] In order to solve the problem of children, especially little girls, being exploited through pageants, society needs to see these pageants for what they are and make them unacceptable in their current forms. Although there are arguably some benefits to pageants, they do not outweigh the cons, and these benefits can be achieved in more constructive ways. Instead of relying on pageants to teach kids manners and poise, perhaps the parents should take responsibility for instilling those characteristics into their children without taking away their childhood. They should teach their children that hard work and a strong character will lead to success, rather than teaching them to exploit their sexuality to get ahead. Though pageants probably cannot be stopped altogether, there should be mandatory regulations that forbid the ridiculous getups and seductive dancing, and if little girls still want to play dress up, they can easily do it at home like millions of little girls have done for hundreds of years.

[10] Exploiting children cannot be justified. It is the responsibility of the adults in society to take care of the kids and protect the well-being of those who cannot yet take care of themselves. Society should not be endorsing an unhealthy activity such as pageants for children. The glitz and glamour of pageant life that appeals to parents should not be worth the emotional and physical health of their offspring. Children should be taught to love and respect themselves as individuals, and *that* is what society and the media should be endorsing. It is time to call for an end to beauty pageants for children and find healthier ways for children to be competitive.

Works Cited

Davidson, Mark. "Is the media to blame for child sex victims?" *USA Today Magazine* Sept. 1997: 60. *Academic Search Premier*. EBSCO. Web. 18 Mar. 2010.

Early, Gerald. "Life with Daughters: Watching the Miss America Pageant". *Kenyon Review* 12.4 (1990): 132-

145. *Academic Search Premier*. EBSCO. Web. 18 Mar. 2010.

Giroux, Henry A. "Nymphet Fantasies: Child Beauty Pageants and the Politics of Innocence". *Social Text* 16.4 (1998): 31-53. *Academic Search Premier*. EBSCO. Web. 18 Mar. 2010.

Hilboldt-Stolley, Lise. "Pretty babies". *Good Housekeeping* 228.2 (1999): 102. *Academic Search Premier*. EBSCO. Web. 22 Mar. 2010.

"Most Famous Pageant". Journal of American History 93.2 (2006): 589-590. *Academic Search Premier*. EBSCO. Web. 19 Mar. 2010.

Wonderlich, Anna, Diann Ackard, and Judith Henderson. "Childhood Beauty Pageant Contestants: Associations with Adult Disordered Eating and Mental Health". *Eating Disorders* 13.3 (2005): 291-301. *Academic Search Premier*. EBSCO. Web. 18 Mar. 2010.

(Source: This essay and the list of works cited are available at https://www.studocu.com/en-ca/document/sheridan-college/composition-and-rhetoric/toulmin-argument-example-excelsior-college/3646453)

Remembering and Understanding

Answer the following questions.

1. According to the text, how are beauty pageants received in American society? Are child beauty pageants received in the same way?

2. What were original child beauty pageants like? What are they like now? Where do they differ significantly?

3. How do the hit television shows of pageant life contribute to the explosion of controversy?

4. How harmful could child beauty pageants be physically?

5. What is the significance of the case of JonBenet Ramsey's murder?

6. How are participation in beauty pageants as children and eating disorders related?

Extensive Reading 4

7. How harmful could child beauty pageants be mentally?

8. According to the author, where lies the solution to this problem of child beauty pageants?

Reasoning and Analyzing

Answer the following questions.

1. What is the claim of this text?

2. In Para. 1, the author raises a rhetorical question—"how can parading children about on stage like show ponies be a positive thing?" and gives a negative answer immediately. What is the effect of applying a rhetorical question here instead of a direct negative statement? Which element—ethos, pathos, logos—does the author apply in this way? What other means in Para. 1 also build that element?

3. What point is Mark Davidson quoted to illustrate in Para. 4? What emotion does the author intend to arouse with his quote? What details in Para. 4 also target the same emotion?

4. What are the features of the media attention on JonBenet Ramsey's murder as quoted by Henry Giroux in Para. 6?

5. The author poses a question at the beginning of Para. 8—"what are their parents thinking?" What do you think their parents are thinking according to the text? Do you think the author is only aiming at answering this question? What other implication does this question carry?

6. The author quotes heavily throughout the whole article and provides sources of the quotes. How could the quotation and sources affect the persuasiveness of the writing? To which rhetorical element(s) do they contribute?

    _____
    _____

7. For the benefits of child beauty pageants in the opposing views, the author does not deny totally, but rather acknowledges to some extent, like "with these supposed benefits" (Para. 8), "there are arguably some benefits to pageants" (Para. 9). Will the reference to opposing views and even a partial acknowledgment reduce the power of the argument? Why or why not?

    _____
    _____

8. Why does the author propose to eliminate the current form of child beauty pageants? What is the underlying logic of this proposal?

    _____
    _____

9. Based on your understanding of the article, how do you think the author would answer the question in the title?

    _____
    _____

Reflecting and Creating

Topics for discussion and writing.

1. The author expresses her strong objection to the current form of child beauty pageants in this article. She seems to be more favorable towards the original form. What is your opinion towards child beauty pageants? Do you think we should have such activities at all, no matter in its original form or its current form? Why or why not?
2. The need to protect children is widely recognized as they are the future of society. The author in this article places the responsibility on the adults in society. What specific measures can you provide to help ensure their healthy growth? Discuss in groups to draw up a list of measures that are feasible in our daily lives.
3. According to the author, TV shows, though they claim to be just documentaries of the life of those child pageant participants, are another kind of exploitation of children. Nowadays, reality shows about children and their lives are quite popular, though those kids do not attend any pageants. Do you think such reality shows of children are also a kind of exploitation? Why or why not?

Extensive Reading 4

Text B I'm a Blind Scientist and Inventor. More Disabled Kids Should Have the Opportunities I Had

 Preparatory Work

Activity 1 What Are the Difficulties?

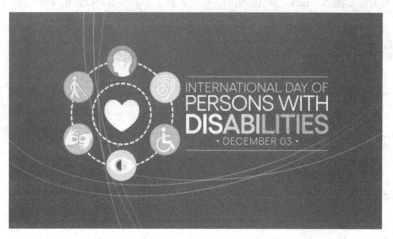

(Source: https://www.winnipegsd.ca/andrewmynarski/_ci/p/24014)

It is generally accepted that it is much more difficult for a blind person to become a scientist and inventor than for a normal person. Where do you think the difficulties might lie? What specific difficulties might they face?

Possible Difficulties

Activity 2 Can You Do It?

Can you imagine what life would be like for a blind person?

You may have a try right now. Keep your eyes closed, take out two different pens, disassemble them and then reassemble them. Or close your eyes, take out all the things in your bag, and then put them back where they belong in the bag.

Do you have any more understanding of their life after this simple try?

My New Understanding of Their Life	

Reading the Text

While the author attributes his success as a blind scientist and inventor to both luck and grit, he contends that exceptionalism shouldn't be a requirement for people with disabilities to flourish in science and math. If an average sighted kid can build a career in STEM, shouldn't an average blind kid be able to, as well?

I'm a Blind Scientist and Inventor. More Disabled Kids Should Have the Opportunities I Had

Joshua Miele[1]

Photo: STEPHEN LAM/AMAZON

(Source: https://people.com/health/dr-joshua-miele-lost-sight-in-acid-attack-blind-more-accessible/)

1　As a little kid, I was fascinated by the inner workings of every device in my family's home. I would spend hours disassembling and reassembling radios, toasters, and other household appliances, trying to figure out how they worked. Some sighted adults marveled at this, but to me, a blind kid exploring the world, it felt perfectly natural. Blindness is a hands-on process.

2　The model kits for steam engines and rockets I received on birthdays didn't come with braille instructions. I'd assemble them by trial and error rather than by following the printed instructions which I couldn't read—how many big screws, how many little screws, four pieces shaped like this, and two pieces shaped like that will form a box. Unfortunately, decades later, very little has changed. Instead of model rockets I now contend with things like IKEA furniture, but assembly is still more like solving a puzzle than a step-by-step process.

3   With this early understanding of disability-related problem solving, I pursued my interests in STEM—science, technology, engineering, and math. My personal story of becoming a successful blind scientist, inventor, accessibility activist, and principal researcher at Amazon is equal parts luck and grit. However, I am once again reminded of the inaccessibility of information, technology, and educational experiences that continue to impede the next generation of disabled students.

4   I was lucky to be born into a privileged, white, educated family who understood my passion for STEM and supported it from childhood. I was lucky to have teachers who made the extra effort to adapt their science and math curricula for a blind kid who had clear passion and potential for STEM. This led me to the University of California, Berkeley, where I studied physics. Even at Berkeley, the birthplace of the Disability Rights Movement, I faced familiar barriers as a blind student learning and living on a campus designed for sighted students. I distinctly remember one of my courses tasked me with building semiconductor circuits, but the campus lacked accessible lab equipment—they didn't expect blind kids to be studying physics. Instead, my lab partners would read the gauges and digital readouts, paid assistants would transcribe circuit diagrams, and I was lucky to find blind mentors who taught me to build some of my own accessible test equipment. Through another blind student, I learned about OutSPOKEN, one of the first commercially available screen readers for computers, which ensured I could access the visual information on the screen.

Image courtesy of Jean Miele

(Source: https://www.pbs.org/newshour/science/how-this-innovator-is-making-sure-the-tech-that-drives-daily-life-doesnt-leave-out-people-with-disabilities)

5   Pursuing an education and career in STEM also required grit to push back against a world that assumed

blind students couldn't succeed in fields where diagrams, maps, equations, and other "visual" media were the ubiquitous tools of record-keeping and communication. But exceptionalism shouldn't be a requirement for people with disabilities to flourish in science and math. If an average sighted kid can build a career in STEM, shouldn't an average blind kid be able to, as well?

6   The struggle of STEM inclusion is still with us. The blind students who attend the electronics and hobby-robotics workshops that I regularly teach usually attend schools that offer similar hands-on learning experiences—but only for sighted students. The blind kids in my workshops are rarely members of the robotics clubs in their schools, not for lack of interest or ability, but because most sighted educators simply can't conceive of blind students being successful in those clubs.

7   Certainly, teachers need training, education, and additional resources to support accessible STEM education, but usually the main thing missing is their ability to see students with disabilities as successful future scientists and engineers. In short, the STEM education of most students with disabilities is a low priority because of ableism—biases and preconceptions that assume disabled students can't succeed.

8   For many years now, educational policy and practice have recognized that STEM fields lack diversity. There are major research programs and intervention efforts to improve the diversity of students who succeed in STEM fields. Academic journals and conferences are dedicated to the topic. Hundreds of millions of dollars are spent on programs to encourage diversity in STEM fields across gender, race, culture, and socioeconomic status, but disability is rarely a significant part of the conversation.

9   From grade schools to tutoring centers and universities, our educational institutions and those who lead them must reimagine their classrooms and campuses. We need schools that support a truly diverse future of engineers, artists, authors, and makers—and that diversity must include disability.

10   Educators can't make this change alone. Just as we need to make sure educational materials and technologies are culturally inclusive, we also need to make sure textbooks, websites, and education software are usable by students with disabilities. Science simulations that are purely visual cannot benefit blind students; deaf students can't learn from uncaptioned videos; electronic textbooks whose fonts cannot be changed or scaled make it hard for dyslexic students to read, and the list goes on and on. We need to help funders, employers, educators, and parents of students with disabilities understand that disability does not preclude success in STEM or in any other career.

11   Like any other meaningful effort towards equity, active participation by community members is essential. We must have educators and leaders with disabilities designing the policies and practices that impact our community's participation in STEM. Designers and engineers with disabilities must have central roles on the teams creating accessible educational materials and technologies used on our campuses. STEM leaders with and without disabilities must make it their responsibility to remove accessibility barriers to

Extensive Reading 4

welcome the next generation of diverse innovators. They must echo the battle cry of the disability rights movement, "Nothing about us without us." Disability inclusion takes place when people with disabilities are "in the room where it happens," from the classroom to the boardroom, and have the power to guide decisions that impact our community and our ability to participate as equals.

12   Now, I invite us all to reexamine the assumptions we have about disability and success and take the opportunity to raise our expectations for the 1 billion people living with disabilities around the globe. Consider the inadvertent accessibility barriers in your personal or professional world that add unnecessary friction to the successful participation of people with disabilities. Ask yourself how you can help remove that friction.

13   Just as our society is learning to recognize and call out racism, sexism, and other biases, we need to become more broadly capable of spotting and eradicating ableism in our personal interactions and institutions. Only then can we move toward an inclusive and accessible world where people with disabilities won't have to be exceptionally lucky and stubborn in order to succeed—in STEM education, in building a career, or in enjoying everyday entertainment. Normalizing disability means changing societal assumptions so that successful people with disabilities, in STEM fields or otherwise, are no longer unusual. Global accessibility and disability inclusion are everyone's business.

(Source: https://www.mbcnschool.org/7-things-you-should-stop-saying-and-doing-to-disabled-people/)

(Source: This article was published on *Time* on Dec. 16, 2022.)

Notes

1. Joshua Miele (1969-) is a blind scientist, inventor, and community leader with decades of experience creating innovative accessibility solutions, including tactile cartography, mobile wayfinding tools, video description technologies, and contribution to accessible STEM education. He won a MacArthur "genius" prize in 2021 and is currently a principal accessibility researcher at Amazon. Joshua Miele was severely burned and left blind after a mentally ill neighbor poured a bottle of acid over his head when he was 4.

Unit 3 Aristotelian Model of Argument

 Remembering and Understanding

Choose the best answer(s) from the choices given based on the text.

1. Which of the following statements about the author is NOT true?

   A. He became blind as a little kid.

   B. He was fascinated by his ability of disassembling and reassembling.

   C. He assembled by trial and error.

   D. He liked to make out the inner workings of household appliances.

2. What does the author think of blindness?

   A. It is natural and should not be an obstacle to success.

   B. It is a hands-on process to success.

   C. It is a trial-and-error process to assembling.

   D. It can be overcome by a step-by-step process.

3. How about the situation for the blind now from when he was a kid?

   A. STEM education now is more friendly and accessible for the blind.

   B. Berkeley grants more rights to the blind.

   C. IKEA furniture provides braille instructions for the blind now.

   D. Accessibility in education and life is not improved much.

4. What are the important factors in the author's success? Choose all that apply.

   A. Family support.

   B. Helpful teachers.

   C. Paid assistants.

   D. Luck.

   E. Grit.

5. Which of the following is the least feasible effort from teachers to improve accessible STEM education for people with disabilities?

   A. Receiving training in teaching disabled students.

   B. Applying materials and resources that are friendly to disabled students.

   C. Initiating another disability rights movement.

   D. Overcoming the assumption that students with disabilities can't be successful scientists and engineers.

6. What kind of school and education is least likely to be supported by the author?

   A. The school and education that are inclusive of students with different cultural backgrounds.

   B. The school and education that are inclusive of students with and without disabilities.

   C. The school and education that provide equal accessibility for students with disabilities.

Extensive Reading 4

D. The school and education that are designed specifically for students with disabilities.

7. Which of the following would NOT be an effective means to improve accessibility for people with disabilities in general?

    A. To help funders, employers, educators, and parents of students with disabilities eradicate ableism.

    B. To have more educators and leaders with disabilities when designing policies and guiding decisions about people with disabilities.

    C. To leave designers and engineers with disabilities the central roles in creating educational materials and technologies.

    D. To help more people with disabilities become lucky and stubborn.

Reasoning and Analyzing

Answer the following questions.

1. What is the common assumption about people with disabilities as suggested by the author?

2. The author asserts that "assembly is still more like solving a puzzle than a step-by-step process"(Para. 2). What is the difference between "solving a puzzle" and "a step-by-step process"? What does the author imply by this comparison?

3. Besides his personal experience, the author also introduces himself as "a successful blind scientist, inventor, accessibility activist, and principal researcher at Amazon" (Para. 3). How could such information help his argument?

4. The author refers repeatedly to his luck in his life and education, for example, "luck and grit" (Para. 3), "I was lucky to be born into ..." (Para. 4), "I was lucky to have teachers who ..." (Para. 4), "I was lucky to find blind mentors who ..." (Para. 4). Why does he emphasize so much on his luck?

5. Why shouldn't exceptionalism "be a requirement for people with disabilities to flourish in science and math" (Para. 5)? What is the underlying logic of this claim?

6. Who is "us" in "Nothing about us without us" (Para. 11)? What does that phrase mean?

7. The author refers to "ableism" again in the last paragraph and juxtaposes it with "racism, sexism, and other biases". What's the effect of this association?

Reflecting and Creating

Topics for discussion and writing.

1. The author of this article proposes equality for people with disabilities and normalizing disabilities. Do you think it would be contradictory to our goodwill to be kind and helpful to them? How should we regard them, as our equals or as people who need help?
2. How to show our goodwill to be kind and friendly to people with disabilities more properly? What specific measures can we take in our daily lives that may be helpful to them?
3. The author relates heavily to his own experience in the text. Does the experience make his argument more convincing, or more personal and therefore reduce its credibility? Why? To what extent do you think one's personal experience can help his argument?

Summary

Self-reflection

Fill out the checklist.

Area	Yes/No?	Notes/Comment
I know what the major elements of the Aristotelian model of argument are.		
I know what ethos is in the Aristotelian model and its effects.		
I know what pathos is in the Aristotelian model and its effects.		

Extensive Reading 4

(continued)

Area	Yes/No?	Notes/Comment
I know what logos means in the Aristotelian model and its importance.		
I know more about the exploitation of children by beauty pageants and the significance of protecting children.		
I have got a deeper understanding of ableism and the necessity of normalizing disability.		

 Value Cultivation

Activity 1 Message Identification

Which of the following statements would the author of Text A most likely agree with? Choose all that apply.

A. Children begin by loving their parents; after a time they judge them; rarely, if ever, do they forgive them.　—Oscar Wilde

B. The greatest legacy one can pass on to one's children and grandchildren is not money or other material things accumulated in one's life, but rather a legacy of character and faith.　—Billy Graham

C. Security is mostly a superstition. It does not exist in nature, nor do the children of men as a whole experience it. Avoiding danger is no safer in the long run than outright exposure. Life is either a daring adventure, or nothing.　—Helen Keller

D. I believe that children are our future. Teach them well and let them lead the way. Show them all the beauty they possess inside.　—Whitney Houston

E. All children are artists. The problem is how to remain an artist once he grows up.　—Pablo Picasso

F. Don't handicap your children by making their lives easy.　—Robert A. Heinlein

G. At the end of the day, the most overwhelming key to a child's success is the positive involvement of parents.　—Jane D. Hull

H. It is easier to build strong children than to repair broken men.　—Frederick Douglass

Activity 2 Translate the Following Excerpt into English.

要弘扬人道主义精神，尊重和保障人权，完善残疾人社会保障制度和关爱服务体系，促进残疾人事业全面发展，支持和鼓励残疾人自强不息，正像一位视障运动员在赛场上所说："我看不清世界，但我想让世界看到我。"

——习近平 2022 年 4 月 8 日在北京冬奥会、冬残奥会总结表彰大会上的讲话

Further Reading

1. "Nymphet Fantasies: Child Beauty Pageants and the Politics of Innocence" by Henry Giroux
2. *Three Days to See* by Hellen Keller
3. *The Story of My Life* by Hellen Keller

Unit 4
Toulmin Model of Argument

Extensive Reading 4

Mastering Critical Reading

Critical thinking involves the analysis and evaluation of arguments. During this process, various types of arguments are encountered, each with their own characteristics and logical structure. Aristotle provides his form of argumentation through his Aristotelian structure, which is particularly effective in persuasive speeches, advertising, or any argument that aims to engage the audience emotionally and intellectually. However, the Toulmin model is beneficial when analyzing or constructing arguments that require a thorough examination of evidence, reasoning, and counterarguments. It is more suitable for academic reading, writing, debates, legal arguments, or any situation where a structured and well-supported argument is needed.

■ **What Is the Toulmin Model?**

The Toulmin model is a framework developed by British philosopher Stephen Toulmin[1] to analyze or construct arguments. It is intended to focus on the justificatory function of argumentation, as Toulmin believed that reasoning is a process of testing and sifting already existing ideas—an act achievable through the process of justification.

(https://www.indeed.com/career-advice/career-development/toulmin-model)

■ **The Shape of the Toulmin Model**

Toulmin asserts in *The Uses of Argument*[2] that the actual components of an argument are more complex than the basic definition suggests. While the conventional definition states that an argument comprises evidence and/or reasons in support of an assertion or claim (whether stated or implied), Toulmin proposes a comprehensive layout consisting of six interrelated components for analyzing arguments. Among these components, three are considered main and necessary, while the remaining three are seen as additional and optional. The chief advantage of the Toulmin model is that it categorizes an argument into these distinct parts. Readers can then analyze and evaluate each part individually to see if the argument is effective.

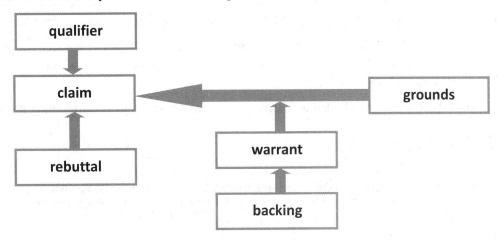

Three "Basics" in the Model

The three basic and main components include the ***claim*** (or thesis or conclusion), which sets up the argument, the ***grounds*** (or data or evidence), providing evidence to support the claim, and the ***warrant*** (or assumption or presupposition), which connects the claim to the grounds. For example:

> **Claim:** Global warming is human-made.
> **Grounds:** Concentrations of greenhouse gases have been increasing significantly since the Industrial Revolution.

In the above argument, there is an essential component that is not stated: the warrant. The warrant plays a crucial role in connecting the claim and the grounds, allowing for a logical progression in the argument. Without a warrant, the grounds cannot be effectively linked to the claim, compromising the overall coherence and validity of the argument. Thus, the inclusion of a warrant is vital to fulfill the logical structure of an argument.

Look at the above sample argument to see what warrant must be accepted to make the argument valid:

> **Claim:** Global warming is human-made.
> **Grounds:** Concentrations of greenhouse gases have been increasing significantly since the Industrial Revolution.
> **Warrant:**

The three primary components of arguments, as discussed in Book 3, have already been covered. Therefore, more space will be dedicated to the discussion of the three optional parts.

Three "Options" in the Model

Extensive Reading 4

The three optional parts in a Toulmin structure are the *backing*, the *qualifier*, and the *rebuttal*.

- ❖ **Backing**: When the author recognizes that the audience does not perceive the warrant of the argument as credible, the author provides additional evidence known as the backing. This serves as supplementary support or justification for the warrant, bolstering the credibility and strengthening the reasoning behind the argument. For example, further support can be added to justify the warrant of the above argument:

> **Claim:** Global warming is human-made.
> **Grounds:** Concentrations of greenhouse gases have been increasing significantly since the Industrial Revolution.
> **Warrant:**
> **Backing:** Greenhouse gases increase the amount of sun's energy that reaches the Earth's surface.

Look at the following argument to see what further support can be given to justify the warrant:

> **Claim:** Our basketball team will win the game tomorrow.
> **Grounds:** Our coach said we would.
> **Warrant:** Our coach's opinion is worthy of belief.
> **Backing:**

- ❖ **Qualifier:** When the evidence or data supporting a claim is not absolute or conclusive, qualifiers can be used to indicate the level of certainty. Qualifiers can take the form of a word, phrase, or statement that acknowledges the conditions or limitations in which the claim may or may not hold true. They add nuance to the argument and acknowledge potential exceptions. By employing different qualifiers, arguments can range from strong assertions to more vague and uncertain statements.

Let us compare the following two pairs of arguments to see how the use of qualifiers changes the level of certainty or scope of the claim:

> **Claim:** Global warming is human-made.
> **Claim:** Global warming is *probably* human-made.

> **Claim:** Our basketball team will win the game tomorrow.
> **Claim:** Our basketball team will win the game tomorrow **unless our forward is injured.**

(Source: https://www.earth.com/news/the-debate-is-over-humans-caused-climate-change/)

- **Rebuttal:** Toulmin contends that for most arguments no solution from either side is absolute and wise debaters should anticipate the ways that opponents can challenge their arguments. The *rebuttal* in a Toulmin model anticipates and addresses opposing viewpoints or objections to the claim. It acknowledges alternative perspectives and strengthens the argument by addressing potential weaknesses.

Read the following arguments closely and examine what counterarguments are addressed and how different approaches are employed in the rebuttals to respond to the counterarguments:

Claim: Global warming is probably (**qualifier**) human-made.   **Rebuttal:** In spite of the natural climate cycles the Earth has experienced in the past, the current rate of warming, largely driven by human activities, is much faster than any natural variation observed in geological records.
Claim: Stricter gun control laws should be implemented.   **Rebuttal:** While it is true that implementing stricter gun control laws may impact law-abiding citizens, it is important to recognize that the primary goal is to enhance public safety and prevent access to firearms by those with criminal intent.
Claim: Animal testing is necessary for medical research to advance.   **Rebuttal:** While alternative methods like computer simulations and in vitro studies have their merits, they are irrelevant to the specific context of complex biological systems that require live organism testing. The ability to observe the effects of a drug or treatment on a living, whole organism is crucial to understanding its efficacy and potential side effects.

Extensive Reading 4

A Checklist for Examining Arguments Based on the Toulmin Model
➢ What statement is the author defending?   ➢ How is the claim qualified?   ➢ In what cases or circumstances would the writer not press his or her claim?   ➢ How does the writer justify the claim?   ➢ Are the grounds really good reasons and relevant to the claim?   ➢ Does the relationship between the claim and the grounds hold up to examination?   ➢ What evidence is offered as further support for the warrant or grounds?   ➢ Is the backing good/reliable/sufficient and relevant to the warrant/grounds it supports?   ➢ Does the author anticipate any potential objections to their point?   ➢ How does the author approach the counterargument?   ➢ Is there any counterargument that the author has not anticipated?   ➢ Are the rebuttals strong and reliable?

💡 Enhancing Your Critical Reading

Read through the piece and break it down into its parts with Toulmin's terms.

Congress should ban animal research because animals are tortured in experiments that have no necessary benefit for humans such as the testing of cosmetics. The well-being of animals is more important than the profits of the cosmetics industry. Only Congress has the authority to make such a law because the corporations can simply move from state to state to avoid legal penalties. Of course, this ban should not apply to medical research. A law to ban all research would go too far. So, the law would probably have to be carefully written to define the kinds of research intended.

Claim	
Grounds	
Warrant	

(continued)

Backing	
Qualifier	
Rebuttal	

Notes

1. Stephen Toulmin (1922-2009) was an English philosopher, logician and educator and one of the founding fathers of modern argumentation theory.
2. *The Uses of Argument* (1958), published in 1958, is considered Toulmin's most influential work, particularly in the field of rhetoric and communication, and in computer science and it still remains in print.

Text A Rising to the Occasion of Our Death

Preparatory Work

(Source: https://www.shutterstock.com/zh/image-photo/euthanasia-yes-no-symbol-male-hand-1883954104)

Extensive Reading 4

Activity 1 Identify Key Concepts and Distinctions

What does euthanasia mean? In articles on this topic, you might have come across such terms as active euthanasia, passive euthanasia, voluntary euthanasia, non-voluntary euthanasia, and involuntary euthanasia. What are their distinctions? Besides, how is euthanasia different from physician-assisted suicide?

Different Concepts of Euthanasia	Meaning of the Concept
active euthanasia	
passive euthanasia	
voluntary euthanasia	
non-voluntary euthanasia	
involuntary euthanasia	
physician-assisted suicide	

Activity 2 About the Movie *You Don't Know Jack*

The movie *You Don't Know Jack* is a 2010 biographical drama film directed by Barry Levinson. It portrays the controversial figure Dr. Jack Kevorkian[1], also known as "Dr. Death". The movie explores the life and actions of Kevorkian, who advocated for euthanasia and became a prominent figure in the euthanasia debate. *You Don't Know Jack* delves into the legal and ethical complexities surrounding end-of-life decisions and the impact of Kevorkian's work on society.

Watch a video about the movie before class and think about the following questions:

❖ How does the movie portray Jack Kevorkian's motivations and beliefs regarding euthanasia?

❖ What boundaries did Jack Kevorkian challenge?

❖ What do you think of the label "Dr. Death" given to Jack Kevorkian by the media and critics?

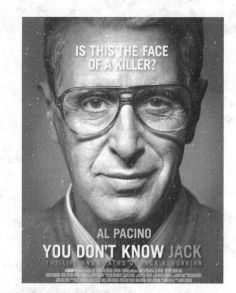

(Source: https://www.imdb.com/title/tt1132623/)

Reading the Text

> Death, as an inevitable part of the human experience, raises questions about the value of life, the preservation of dignity, and the autonomy of individuals facing debilitating illnesses. Euthanasia, the act of intentionally ending a person's life to alleviate suffering, poses ethical dilemmas and evokes strong emotions.

Rising to the Occasion of Our Death
William May[2]

1 For many parents, a Volkswagen van is associated with putting children to sleep on a camping trip. Jack Kevorkian, a Detroit pathologist, has now linked the van with the veterinarian's meaning of "putting to sleep". Kevorkian conducted a dinner interview with Janet Elaine Adkins, a 54-year-old Alzheimer's patient, and her husband and then agreed to help her commit suicide in his VW wan. Kevorkian pressed beyond the more generally accepted practice of passive euthanasia (allowing a patient to die by withholding or withdrawing treatment) to active euthanasia (killing for mercy).

2 Kevorkian, moreover, did not comply with the strict regulations that govern active euthanasia in, for example, the Netherlands. Holland requires that death be imminent (Adkins had beaten her son in tennis just a few days earlier); it demands a more professional review of the medical evidence and the patient's resolution than a dinner interview with a physician (who is stranger and who does not treat patients) permits; and it calls for the final, endorsing signatures of two doctors.

3 So Kevorkian-bashing is easy. But the question remains: Should we develop a judicious, regulated social policy permitting voluntary euthanasia for the terminally ill? Some moralists argue that the distinction between allowing to die and killing for

(Source: https://www.amazon.com/Dr-Death-Jack-Kevorkians-Rx/dp/0811907821)

mercy is petty quibbling over technique. Since the patient in any event dies—whether by acts of omission or commission—the route to death doesn't really matter. The way modern procedures have made dying at the hands of the experts and their machines such a prolonged and painful business has further fueled the euthanasia movement[3], which asserts not simply the right to die but the right to be killed.

4 But other moralists believe that there is an important moral distinction between allowing to die and mercy killing. The euthanasia movement, these critics contend, wants to engineer death rather than face

dying. Euthanasia would bypass dying to make one dead as quickly as possible. It aims to relieve suffering by knocking out the interval between life and death. It solves the problem of suffering by eliminating the sufferer.

(Source: https://www.dignityindying.org.uk/)

5   The impulse behind the euthanasia movement is understandable in an age when dying has become such an inhumanly endless business. But the movement may fail to appreciate our human capacity to rise to the occasion of our death. The best death is not always the sudden death. Those forewarned of death and given time to prepare for it have time to engage in acts of reconciliation. Also, advanced grieving by those about to be bereaved may ease some of their pain. Psychiatrists have observed that those who lose a loved one accidentally have a more difficult time recovering from the loss than those who have suffered through an extended period of illness before the death. Those who have lost a close relative by accident are more likely to experience what Geoffrey Gorer[4] has called limitless grief. The community, moreover, may need its aged and dependent, its sick and its dying, and the virtues which they sometimes evince—the virtues of humility, courage, and patience—just as much as the community needs the virtues of justice and love manifest in the agents of care.

6   On the whole, our social policy should allow terminal patients to die, but it should not regularize killing for mercy. Such a policy would recognize and respect that moment in illness when it no longer makes sense to bend every effort to cure or to prolong life and when one must allow patients to do their own dying. This policy seems most consonant with the obligations of the community to care and of the patient to finish his or her course.

(Source: https://www.holmanwebb.com.au/blog/274/euthanasia-what-is-the-law-in-australia)

7   Advocates of active euthanasia appeal to the principle of patient autonomy—as the use of the phrase "voluntary euthanasia" indicates. But emphasis on the patient's right to determine his or her destiny often harbors an extremely naive view of the uncoerced nature of the decision. Patients who plead to be put to death hardly make unforced decisions if the terms and conditions under which they receive care already nudge them in the direction of the exit. If the elderly have stumbled around in their apartments, alone and frightened for years, or if they have spent years warehoused in geriatrics barracks[5], then the decision to be killed for mercy hardly reflects an uncoerced decision. The alternative may be so wretched as to push patients toward this escape. It is a huge irony and, in some cases, hypocrisy to talk suddenly about a compassion for many years. Otherwise we kill for compassion only to reduce the demands on our compassion. This statement does not charge a given doctor or family member with impure motives. I am concerned here not with the individual case but with the cumulative impact of a social policy.

8   I can, to be sure, imagine rare circumstances in which I hope I would have the courage to kill for mercy—when the patient is utterly beyond human care, terminal, and in excruciating pain. A neurosurgeon once showed a group of physicians and an ethicist the picture of a Vietnam casualty who had lost all four limbs in a landmine explosion. The catastrophe had reduced the soldier to a trunk with his face transfixed in horror. On the battlefield I would hope that I would have the courage to kill the sufferer with mercy.

9   But hard cases do not always make good laws or wise social policies. Regularized mercy killings would too quickly relieve the community of its obligation to provide good care. Further, we should not always expect the law to provide us with full protection and coverage for what, in rare circumstances, we may morally need to do. Sometimes the moral life calls us out into a no-man's-land where we cannot expect total security and protection under the law. But no one said that the moral life is easy.

(Source: This article was published in *The Christian Century* in July, 1990.)

Extensive Reading 4

Notes

1. **Jack Kevorkian** (1928-2011)**,** also known as "Dr. Death", was a controversial figure in the United States during the 1990s. Kevorkian was a pathologist and euthanasia advocate. He developed a euthanasia device called the "Mercitron" and assisted numerous terminally ill patients in ending their lives. His actions sparked intense debate about the ethics and legality of euthanasia, physician-assisted suicide, and end-of-life care. Ultimately, Kevorkian's actions led to his legal troubles and imprisonment.
2. **William F. May** (1927-2023) was an American ethicist, academic, theologian, and ordained Presbyterian minister, serving as a distinguished Professor of Ethics at Southern Methodist University. He was known for his work on medical ethics, particularly in the areas of end-of-life care, reproductive ethics, and the ethics of human experimentation. May's writings, including *Testing the Medical Covenant: Active Euthanasia and Health Care Reform* (1996) and *The Patient's Ordeal* (1991), often explore the moral dimensions of these issues and emphasize the importance of ethical considerations in healthcare decision-making.
3. **The euthanasia movement** in America refers to the ongoing advocacy for the legalization and acceptance of euthanasia or physician-assisted suicide (PAS) in certain circumstances. The modern euthanasia movement in America gained momentum in the late 20th century, with notable figures such as Jack Kevorkian bringing attention to the issue. Several organizations, such as Compassion & Choices, Death with Dignity National Center, Hemlock Society, have been at the forefront of advocating for the right to die with dignity and the legalization of euthanasia or physician-assisted suicide (PAS).
4. **Geoffrey Gorer** (1905-1985) was an English anthropologist, sociologist, and writer known for his studies on a wide range of topics, including social anthropology, cultural norms, sexuality, and death. He made significant contributions to the field of anthropology and social sciences during his career.
5. **Geriatrics barracks** typically refer to dedicated facilities or wards within hospitals or medical centers that provide specialized care for elderly patients. These units are designed to address the unique medical, social, and emotional needs of older individuals.

Remembering and Understanding

Activity 1 Identify and Synthesize Information

Kevorkian was a controversial figure for his practices of euthanasia. Holland is the first country in the world legalizing euthanasia. Fill in the blanks to find out Kevorkian's non-compliance with the regulations in the Netherlands.

Kevorkian's Practice of Euthanasia
Jack Kevorkian conducted 1._____ with Janet Elaine Adkins, a 54-year-old Alzheimer's patient, and her husband, and agreed to help her 2._____ in his VW van.

Holland's Requirements for Active Euthanasia
The Netherlands has 3._____ for active euthanasia compared to Kevorkian's practices, including the requirement of 4._____, a more 5._____ of medical evidence and patient's resolution, and the 6._____ of two doctors.

Activity 2 Multiple-choice Questions

1. What is Jack Kevorkian's role in the context of euthanasia?

    A. He is a patient suffering from Alzheimer's.

    B. He is a pathologist associated with Detroit hospitals.

    C. He is a veterinarian who specializes in euthanasia.

    D. He is a physician who engages in euthanasia practices.

2. The dispute among moralists concerning euthanasia is mainly attributed to _____.

    A. differences in medical procedures and techniques

    B. conflicting views on patient autonomy

    C. divided perspectives on the distinction between allowing to die and mercy killing

    D. disagreements over the role of experts and machines in the dying process

3. What do critics of euthanasia argue regarding the aim of the euthanasia movement?

    A. The euthanasia movement aims to engineer death rather than face dying.

    B. The euthanasia movement seeks to provide relief from suffering by prolonging the interval between life and death.

    C. The euthanasia movement wants to eliminate the sufferer to solve the problem of suffering.

    D. The euthanasia movement aims to bypass dying and make one dead as slowly as possible.

4. According to the essay, what is the potential benefit of forewarning patients about their impending death?

    A. Patients are more likely to recover from the loss of a loved one.

    B. Patients experience less pain during the dying process.

    C. Patients have time to engage in acts of reconciliation.

    D. Patients are more likely to make uncoerced decisions about euthanasia.

5. What is the author's stance regarding social policy on euthanasia?

    A. Social policy should regularize killing for mercy.

    B. Social policy should recognize the moment when patients should do their own dying.

    C. Social policy should emphasize patient autonomy in all cases.

    D. Social policy should focus on providing total security and protection under the law.

6. The author believes killing for mercy may be justified when _____.

Extensive Reading 4

A. a patient is beyond human care, terminal, and in excruciating pain

B. the euthanasia movement advocates for it

C. strict regulations regarding active euthanasia are followed

D. passive euthanasia has failed as an option

Reasoning and Analyzing

Toulmin Analysis of the Argument

Identify the six components in the argument based on the following questions:

❖ What is the author's view on euthanasia?

❖ How is the claim qualified?

❖ In what circumstances would the author not press his claim?

❖ How does the author justify his claim?

❖ How are the grounds connected to the claim?

❖ Is there evidence offered as further support for the warrant or grounds?

❖ Does the author anticipate any potential objections to his view?

❖ How does the author address the counterargument?

The Case: Rising to the Occasion of Our Death			
Claim: Qualifier? Exceptions?			
Ground:	Ground:	Ground:	Ground:
Warrant:	Warrant:	Warrant:	Warrant:
Backing:	Backing:	Backing:	Backing:
Objection:	Objection:	Objection:	Objection:
Rebuttal:	Rebuttal:	Rebuttal:	Rebuttal:

Reflecting and Creating

Topics for discussion and writing.

1. How does the case of Jack Kevorkian challenge the distinction between allowing to die and killing for mercy? Do you agree that the route to death doesn't really matter since the patient ultimately dies?
2. The article mentions the impulse behind the euthanasia movement and the human capacity to rise to the occasion of death. How do you interpret the notion of "the best death" and the role of preparation, reconciliation, and advanced grieving in the dying process? Do you think active euthanasia is not "the best death" because it leads to "the sudden death", leaving the terminally ill no time for preparation, reconciliation, and advanced grieving in the dying process?
3. The author raises concerns about the uncoerced nature of decisions for euthanasia and the potential influence of care conditions. How might the circumstances and environment in which patients receive care impact their choices? Do you agree that such decisions may not always be truly unforced?
4. In considering rare circumstances where mercy killing may be justified, the author highlights the complexity of formulating social policies based on hard cases. What are the risks and implications of regularizing mercy killings?

Text B In Defense of Voluntary Euthanasia

Preparatory Work

Activity 1 Interpret the Cartoon

(Source: https://natlib.govt.nz/records/23194021)

Extensive Reading 4

Look at the cartoon and consider the following questions:

❖ What is the man experiencing?

❖ What does the woman suggest?

❖ What can you infer about their stance on the issue of euthanasia?

❖ What is the attitude of the cartoonist?

Activity 2 Movie Review: *The Sea Inside*

Have you seen or heard of the movie *The Sea Inside* (original title: *Mar adentro*)? It is a Spanish film directed by Alejandro Amenábar and released in 2004. It won numerous awards, including the 77th Academy Award for Best Foreign Language Film. The movie tells the real-life story of Ramón Sampedro, a Spanish man who became a quadriplegic after a diving accident and fought for his right to die with dignity.

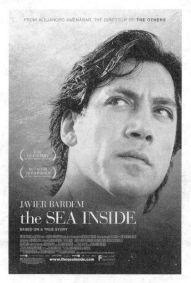

(Source: https://www.imdb.com/title/tt0369702/)   (Source: https://tvtropes.org/pmwiki/pmwiki.php/Film/TheSeaInside)

Watch a clip of the movie and read the following dialogue between Ramón and Julia, a lawyer, who becomes involved in Ramón's case and helps him in his fight for euthanasia.

Julia: Why choose death?

Ramón Sampedro: Well, I want to die because I feel that a life for me in this state has no dignity. I understand that other quadriplegics may take offense to my saying there's no dignity in this, but I'm not trying to judge anyone. Who am I to judge those who choose life? So don't judge me or anyone who wants to help me die.

Julia: You think someone will help?

Ramón Sampedro: Well, that depends on the *powers* that be. They'll have to overcome their fear. But hey, it's really no big deal. Death has always been with us and always will be. It catches up with all of us.

Everyone. It's part of us. So why are they shocked because I choose to die, as if it were contagious?

Julia: If this goes to court, they'll ask why you haven't explored all alternatives. Why refuse a wheelchair?

Ramón Sampedro: Accepting a wheelchair would be like accepting the scraps of the freedom I lost. Think about this: You're sitting there, three feet away. What's three feet? An insignificant distance for any human being. But for me, those three feet that keep me from reaching you, from touching you, are an impossible journey. Just an illusion. A fantasy. That's why I want to die.

Share your ideas on the following questions:

❖ Why does Ramón choose to die?

❖ Why does he ask not to be judged for his desire to die?

❖ What might the "powers" refer to?

❖ Why does he refuse a wheelchair?

❖ Do you support Ramón's choice for euthanasia after learning about his story?

Reading the Text

> In the realm of medical ethics and end-of-life care, the contentious issue of voluntary euthanasia stands at the forefront, sparking intense debates and raising profound questions about autonomy, compassion, and the boundaries of medical intervention. Should a person be allowed to decide when they want to die?

In Defense of Voluntary Euthanasia
Sidney Hook[1]

1   A few short years ago, I lay at the point of death. A congestive heart failure was treated for diagnostic purposes by an angiogram that triggered a stroke. Violent and painful hiccups, uninterrupted for several days and nights, prevented the ingestion of food. My left side and one of my vocal cords became paralyzed. Some form of pleurisy set in, and I felt I was drowning in a sea of slime. At one point, my heart stopped beating; just as I lost consciousness, it was thumped back into action again. In one of my lucid intervals during those days of agony, I asked my physician to discontinue all life-supporting services or show me how to do it. He refused and predicted that someday I would appreciate the unwisdom of my request.

2   A month later, I was discharged from the hospital. In six months, I regained the use of my limbs, and although my voice still lacks its old resonance and carrying power I no longer croak like a frog. There remain some minor disabilities and I am restricted to a rigorous, low-sodium diet. I have resumed my writing and research.

³ My experience can be and has been cited as an argument against honoring requests of stricken patients to be gently eased out of their pain and life. I cannot agree. There are two main reasons. As an octogenarian, there is a reasonable likelihood that I may suffer another "cardiovascular accident" or worse. I may not even be in a position to ask for the surcease of pain. It seems to me that I have already paid my dues to death—indeed, although time has softened my memories they are vivid enough to

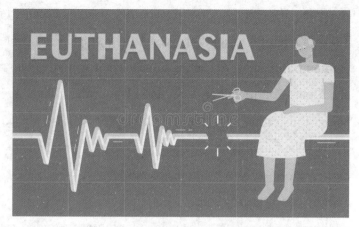

(Source: https://www.dreamstime.com/vector-illustration-man-who-decided-to-use-euthanasia-colorful-depicts-cuts-off-pulse-his-life-scissors-thus-image173619582)

justify my saying that I suffered enough to warrant dying several times over. Why run the risk of more?

⁴ Secondly, I dread imposing on my family and friends another grim round of misery similar to the one my first attack occasioned.

⁵ My wife and children endured enough for one lifetime. I know that for them the long days and nights of waiting, the disruption of their professional duties and their own familial responsibilities counted for nothing in their anxiety for me. In their joy at my recovery they have been forgotten. Nonetheless, to visit another prolonged spell of helpless suffering on them as my life ebbs away, or even worse, if I linger on into a comatose senility, seems altogether gratuitous.

⁶ But what, it may be asked, of the joy and satisfaction of living, of basking in the sunshine, listening to music, watching one's grandchildren growing into adolescence, following the news about the fate of freedom in a troubled world, playing with ideas, writing one's testament of wisdom and folly for posterity? Is not all that one endured, together with the risk of its recurrence, an acceptable price for the multiple satisfactions that are still open even to a person of advanced years?

⁷ Apparently those who cling to life no matter what, think so. I do not.

⁸ The zest and intensity of these experiences are no longer what they used to be. I am not vain enough to delude myself that I can in the few remaining years make an important discovery useful for mankind or can lead a social movement or do anything that will be historically eventful, no less event-making. My autobiography, which describes a record of intellectual and political experiences of some historical value, already much too long, could be posthumously published. I have had my fill of joys and sorrows and am not greedy for more life. I have always thought that a test of whether one had found happiness in one's life is whether one would be willing to relive it—whether, if it were possible, one would accept the opportunity to be born again.

9   Having lived a full and relatively happy life, I would cheerfully accept the chance to be reborn, but certainly not to be reborn again as an infirm octogenarian. To some extent, my views reflect what I have seen happen to the aged and stricken who have been so unfortunate as to survive crippling paralysis. They suffer, and impose suffering on others, unable even to make a request that their torment be ended.

10 I am mindful too of the burdens placed upon the community, with its rapidly diminishing resources, to provide the adequate and costly services necessary to sustain the lives of those whose days and nights are spent on mattress graves of pain. A better use could be made of these resources to increase the opportunities and qualities of life for the young. I am not denying the moral obligation the community has to look after its disabled and aged. There are times, however, when an individual may find it pointless to insist on the fulfillment of a legal and moral right.

11 What is required is no great revolution in morals but an enlargement of imagination and an intelligent evaluation of alternative uses of community resources.

12 Long ago, Seneca[2] observed that "the wise man will live as long as he ought, not as long as he can". One can envisage hypothetical circumstances in which one has a duty to prolong one's life despite its costs for the sake of others, but such circumstances are far removed from the ordinary prospects we are considering. If wisdom is rooted in knowledge of the alternatives of choice, it must be reliably informed of the state one is in and its likely outcome. Scientific medicine is not infallible, but it is the best we have. No rational person would forego relief from prolonged agony merely on the chance that a miraculous cure might presently be at hand. Each one should be permitted to make his own choice—especially when no one else is harmed by it.

(Source: https://nirvanic.co/seneca-quotes-stoicism/

13 The responsibility for the decision, whether deemed wise or foolish, must be with the chooser.

(Source: This article was first published in *The New York Times* on March 1, 1987.)

Extensive Reading 4

> **Notes**
>
> 1. **Sidney Hook** (1902-1989) was an American philosopher and social critic known for his contributions to pragmatism, political philosophy, and the philosophy of history. Hook was introduced to John Dewey's ideas while studying at Columbia University, where Dewey was a prominent figure and a leading proponent of pragmatism. Hook was a prolific writer, and his works spanned a wide range of topics in philosophy, politics, and social criticism, such as, *The Metaphysics of Pragmatism* (1927), *The Hero in History: A Study in Limitation and Possibility* (1943), *Out of Step: An Unquiet Life in the 20th Century* (1987), etc.
> 2. **Seneca**, also known as Seneca the Younger (4 BC - AD 65), was a prominent Stoic philosopher, statesman, and playwright in ancient Rome. "No philosopher more than Seneca recommended so enthusiastically and vigorously, nor practiced so decisively, taking control of death by choosing it in the form of suicide." His philosophical writings have had a lasting impact on Western thought and continue to be studied and appreciated today.

 ## Remembering and Understanding

Activity 1 Identify and Synthesize Information

In the first two paragraphs, the author shares his own story of suffering and recovery from a life-threatening health crisis. How severe was this crisis and how well did he recover from it? Complete the following table by filling in the blanks.

The Harrowing Experience of Being on the Brink of Death
1. The crisis started with a _____, which was treated with an angiogram.
2. The angiogram triggered a _____.
3. He suffered from _____ that lasted for several days and nights, making it impossible to _____.
4. His left side and one of their vocal cords became _____.
5. _____, accompanied by a sensation of drowning, further added to his suffering.
6. At one point, his heart _____, but it was revived just as he lost consciousness.
The Recovery from the Crisis
7. A month later, the author was _____ from the hospital.
8. Over the course of six months, he gradually regained the use of his _____, although his voice still lacked its original _____.
9. He also faced minor _____ and had to follow a rigorous, low-sodium _____.
10. Despite these challenges, he was able to resume his _____ and research.

Activity 2 Answer the Following Questions

1. What did the author ask his physician to do while he was suffering severely from a "cardiovascular accident"? Why does he ask for it?
   _____
   _____

2. What did his physician think of his request?
   _____
   _____

3. How did the author's family and friends experience his first attack and subsequent recovery?
   _____
   _____

4. According to the author, what is an unacceptable price for the multiple satisfactions of life?
   _____
   _____

5. Does the author believe his remaining years hold the potential for making historically significant contributions?
   _____
   _____

6. What does the author suggest could be a better use of community resources?
   _____
   _____

7. What is the author's implied message regarding individual autonomy and decision-making?
   _____
   _____

8. Where does the author believe the responsibility for the decision lies?
   _____
   _____

Reasoning and Analyzing

Activity 1 Toulmin Analysis of the Argument

Identify the six components in the argument based on the following questions:

- What is the author's view on euthanasia?
- How is the claim qualified?

Extensive Reading 4

- In what circumstances would the author not press his claim?
- How does the author justify his claim?
- How are the grounds connected to the claim?
- Is there evidence offered as further support for the warrant or grounds?
- Does the author anticipate any potential objections to his view?
- How does the author address the counterargument?

Claim	
Grounds	
Warrant	
Backing	
Qualifier	
Rebuttal	

Activity 2 Answer the Following Questions

1. How does the author's personal experience shape his perspective on voluntary euthanasia?

　

　

2. Why does Sidney Hook believe that his experience cannot be used as an argument against honoring requests for euthanasia?

　

　

3. What does the author mean by saying "I have already paid my dues to death" (Para. 3)?

　

　

4. Among a range of activities that can bring joy and satisfaction in one's life, what do these pursuits, "following the news about the fate of freedom in a troubled world, playing with ideas and writing one's

testament of wisdom and folly for posterity"(Para. 6), reflect?

_____
_____

5. How does the author view the potential joys and satisfactions of life in his advanced years? What tone does the author adopt towards the potential for making significant contributions in his remaining years?

_____
_____

6. What is the underlying message conveyed by the author's statement that "a test of whether one had found happiness in one's life is whether one would be willing to relive it"(Para. 8)?

_____
_____

7. How does the author address the concerns about burdening the community's resources with healthcare for the disabled and aged?

_____
_____

8. How does the metaphor "mattress graves of pain" (Para. 10) emphasize the suffering experienced by those in need?

_____
_____

 Reflecting and Creating

Activity 1 Evaluate the Effectiveness of the Arguments

Both of the two articles in this Unit address the issue of euthanasia. While Hook defends voluntary euthanasia, May argues terminal patients can only be allowed to die, but cannot be killed for mercy. Review the six components of the Toulmin model that make up each of the two arguments and evaluate their effectiveness based on the following questions:

- ❖ Is the claim clear or ambiguous?
- ❖ Are the grounds as good as the values they evoke?
- ❖ Are the grounds relevant to the claim?
- ❖ Does the warrant convey good values or beliefs?
- ❖ Does the warrant fulfill the validity of the argument?
- ❖ Does the author offer relevant, reliable and sufficient evidence in further support of the warrant and grounds?

Extensive Reading 4

❖ Is there any counterargument that the author has not anticipated?

❖ How strong and convincing are the rebuttals?

Activity 2 Role-play: Explore Diverse Perspectives on Euthanasia

1. Divide the class into 5 groups.

2. Assign each group a specific role to play during the activity. Here are the suggested roles for the 5 groups:

Group	The Role Each Group Plays
Group 1	**Patient:** A terminally ill individual who is considering active euthanasia as an option
Group 2	**Family Member:** A close family member or caregiver of the patient, who may have concerns or reservations about active euthanasia
Group 3	**Medical Professional:** A healthcare provider who must consider the ethical, legal, and professional implications of assisting in a patient's death
Group 4	**Ethicist:** A person specializing in ethics who can provide guidance and explore moral dilemmas related to euthanasia
Group 5	**Legal Expert:** A legal professional who can explain the existing laws and regulations surrounding euthanasia

3. Provide each group with a set of questions to encourage them to think critically about the perspectives, concerns, and arguments of their assigned role. Here are some example questions:

Group	Example Questions for Each Group
Group 1	What factors might lead a terminally ill person to consider euthanasia? What are the potential benefits and drawbacks of having access to euthanasia? How might personal values and beliefs influence a patient's decision?
Group 2	What concerns or reservations might a family member have about euthanasia? How can emotional and ethical conflicts arise within the family in relation to this decision? What alternative options might be considered to address the patient's suffering?
Group 3	What ethical considerations come into play when considering euthanasia? How do medical professionals balance their duty to provide care with the patient's autonomy? What safeguards should be in place to ensure the decision-making process is thorough and informed?
Group 4	What are some of the moral dilemmas associated with euthanasia? How can ethical frameworks and principles guide decision-making in these cases? Are there any potential risks or unintended consequences of legalizing euthanasia?

(continued)

Group	Example Questions for Each Group
Group 5	What are the current legal frameworks and regulations surrounding euthanasia in different countries and districts? How can the law balance individual autonomy with the need for safeguards and oversight? What are some key legal considerations in ensuring the fair and ethical implementation of euthanasia?

4. After the group discussions, reconvene as a class and provide an opportunity for each group to share a summary of their discussions and any key insights they gained.

Summary

Self-reflection

Fill out the checklist.

Area	Yes/No?	Notes/Comment
I know the definition of the Toulmin model.		
I know the distinction between Aristotelian model and Toulmin model.		
I know the three basic and three optional components of a Toulmin argument.		
I know the relationship between the six components.		
I know how the three basic elements make up the core of an argument and three optional ones strengthen it.		
I know how to use the Toumin model to evaluate arguments.		
I have got a comprehensive and deeper understanding of euthanasia.		

Extensive Reading 4

 Value Cultivation

Activity 1 Quote Sharing

Here are three Chinese quotes about the significance of life and death. Paraphrase them in your own words and then match them with their corresponding English translation.

1. 人之所欲，生甚矣；人之所恶，死甚矣；然而人有从生成死者，非不欲生而欲死也，不可以生而可以死也。——《荀子·正名》
2. 夫大块载我以形，劳我以生，佚我以老，息我以死，故善吾生者，乃所以善吾死也。——《庄子·大宗师》
3. 人于生死念头，本从生身命根上带来，故不易去。若于此处见得破，透得过，此心全体方是流行无碍，方是尽性至命之学。——《王阳明全集·传习录下》

A. Nature endows me with a physical form, labor gives value to my life, old age provides me with comfort, and death grants me rest. Therefore, those who consider life is something good will be able to handle death appropriately.

B. The notion of life and death in human beings originates from the very root of their existence, and thus it cannot be easily discarded. If one can truly understand and penetrate this, the entirety of the mind will be unobstructed, and this is the ultimate wisdom of fully realizing one's nature and destiny.

C. There is no desire stronger than the desire to live, and there is no aversion stronger than the aversion to death. However, some people choose to give up their lives, not because they desire death, but because they believe that the meaning of death outweighs that of life.

Activity 2 Appreciate "Do Not Go Gentle into That Good Night"

"Do Not Go Gentle into That Good Night" is a poem by Dylan Thomas[1] dedicated to his father. Listen to the recitation of the poem and share your understanding of the first three lines based on the following questions:

Do not go gentle into that good night,
Old age should burn and rave at close of day;
Rage, rage against the dying of the light.

Do Not Go Gentle Into That Good Night

Do not go gentle into that good night,
Old age should burn and rave at close of day;
Rage, rage against the dying of the light.

Though wise men at their end know dark is right,
Because their words had forked no lightening they
Do not go gentle into that good night.

Good men, the last wave by, crying how bright
Their frail deeds might have danced in a green bay,
Rage, rage against the dying of the light.

Wild men who caught and sang the sun in flight,
And learn, too late, they grieved it on its way,
Do not go gentle into that good night.

Grave men, near death, who see with blinding sight
Blind eyes could blaze like meteors and be gay,
Rage, rage against the dying of the light.

And you, my father, there on the sad height,
Curse, bless, me now with your fierce tears, I pray.
Do not go gentle into that good night.
Rage, rage against the dying of the light.

Dylan Thomas

- ❖ What does "that good night" and "the light" refer to respectively?
- ❖ What emotions does the poet evoke in the choice of such words as "burn", "rave" and "rage"?
- ❖ What attitude does the poet think we should hold towards "that good night" and "the light"? Do you agree with him?

Extensive Reading 4

Notes

1. **Dylan Thomas** (1914-1953) was a renowned Welsh poet. He is best known for his lyrical and often evocative poetry, marked by rich imagery and musicality. Thomas's works explore themes of love, death, identity, and the power of language. One of his most famous works is the poem "Do Not Go Gentle into That Good Night", in which he passionately urges his father, and by extension all individuals, to fight against the inevitability of death. The poem is a powerful reflection on mortality and the will to live.

 Further Reading

1. *Being Mortal* by Atul Gawande
2. "The Future of the Right-to-Die Movement" by Tierney Sneed
3. "The Final Journey" by Charlotte Naughton

Unit 5
Nonrational Appeals

Extensive Reading 4

Mastering Critical Reading

When discussing concepts such as definition, evidence, deduction, and induction, we primarily focus on rational appeals. Nonetheless, an individual's perspective on reality and truth is molded by a mix of rational and nonrational influences. It is crucial to recognize that the lack of persuasion by an argument does not necessarily imply a logical flaw within the argument. Personal beliefs and subjective factors, which may not be grounded in reason, also play a significant role in shaping one's convictions and can impact the process of persuasion.

■ **What Are Nonrational Appeals?**

Rather than relying solely on logical reasoning and evidence, nonrational appeals in arguments encompass a range of persuasive techniques that aim to tap into people's emotions, values, desires, personal experiences, etc. These appeals recognize the power of human psychology and seek to connect with individuals on a deeper and more personal level. Common nonrational appeals include:

■ **Appeal to Emotions:** It aims to evoke in the audience specific emotions of joy, fear, anger, nostalgia, or empathy to support a particular viewpoint or action.

(Source: https://www.youtube.com/watch?v=sjzX7UemMb4)

Read the following argument about animal rights:

> ? Imagine the life of an innocent, defenseless animal trapped in a tiny cage, deprived of natural behaviors, and subjected to cruel experiments for the sake of human progress. Picture their pain, fear, and suffering, all in the name of scientific advancement. These sentient beings, capable of feeling love, joy, and pain, deserve our compassion and protection.
>
> *How is the appeal to emotions used to influence the audience?*

Emotional appeals can be effective in engaging an audience, capturing attention, and influencing attitudes or behaviors. However, it's important to use emotional appeals responsibly and cautiously, ensuring that they are not manipulative, deceitful, or exploiting vulnerable emotions. They should be supported by sound reasoning, evidence, and a genuine concern for the audience.

- **Appeal to Ethics:** It appeals to the audience's sense of right and wrong, morality, or values. They often invoke concepts of justice, fairness, integrity, or duty to persuade the audience to accept a particular viewpoint or course of action.

Read the following paragraph about euthanasia:

(Source: https://marketblazer.com/blog/how-to-use-manipulation-in-marketing-ethically/)

Extensive Reading 4

> **?** On the whole, our social policy should allow terminal patients to die, but it should not regularize killing for mercy. Such a policy would recognize and respect that moment in illness when it no longer makes sense to bend every effort to cure or to prolong life and when one must allow patients to do their own dying. This policy seems most consonant with the obligations of the community to care and of the patient to finish his or her course.
> *How is the appeal to ethics used to influence the audience?*

Ethical appeals can be effective in persuading an audience when used responsibly and in alignment with genuine ethical considerations. However, it's important to critically evaluate ethical appeals to ensure they are not manipulative, fallacious, or based on biased or subjective moral judgments.

■ **Irony, Sarcasm and Satire:** Besides emotional and ethical appeals, relying on irony, satire, and sarcasm can be effective in engaging the audience and influencing their perception or attitudes towards a particular subject or viewpoint.

Irony	Irony is the use of words or expressions to convey a meaning that is the *opposite* of the literal interpretation, often to highlight contradictions or create a humorous effect. For example, on a rainy day, someone remarks, "What *perfect* weather we're having!"
Sarcasm	Sarcasm involves using irony to express contempt, mock, or belittle someone or something. For example, when John spills coffee on his shirt, Bob says, "Nice job, John!"
Satire	Satire employs humor, irony, or exaggeration to critique or ridicule societal issues, institutions, or individuals. Mark Twain[1] is known for his wit and satire. He once remarked: "Man was made at the end of the week's work, when God was tired."

Here's a short excerpt from "A Modest Proposal" by Jonathan Swift[2]:

> **?** I have been assured by a very knowing American of my acquaintance in London that a young healthy child well nursed is at a year old a most delicious, nourishing, and wholesome food, whether stewed, roasted, baked, or boiled; and I make no doubt that it will equally serve in a fricassee or a ragout.
> *How are such devices as irony, satire, or sarcasm used to influence the audience?*

Unit 5 Nonrational Appeals

While these devices may not rely on logical reasoning or evidence in a direct manner, they can be effective in conveying a message, challenging prevailing views, or stimulating critical thinking. However, it is important to note that the impact of these appeals can vary depending on the audience's familiarity with the context, cultural references, and the overall tone employed.

(Source: https://www.cartoonstock.com/directory/c/climate_irony.asp)

These nonrational appeals can be powerful tools for persuasion, as they can evoke emotional responses, entertain the audience, or expose flaws in an argument. However, it's important to use them legitimately and in conjunction with logical reasoning and evidence to provide a well-rounded and compelling argument. Besides, it's necessary to consider the context and potential impact they may have on the audience. Overuse or misuse of these appeals can undermine the credibility of the argument, and hinder effective communication.

Enhancing Your Critical Reading

Enjoy the cartoons. Most political cartoons in newspapers and magazines demonstrate the use of nonrational appeals. Analyze the following cartoons to see how nonrational appeals are used in each to help the author achieve their purpose.

(Credit: Li Min[2])

(Credit: Luo Jie[3])

Extensive Reading 4

(Credit: Phil Hands[4])

(Credit: Matt Wuerker[5])

What the Cartoon Is Saying	Nonrational Appeals Used to Achieve the Purpose

Notes

1. **Mark Twain** (1835-1910) was an American writer, humorist, and lecturer. Celebrated for his wit, humor, and satire, Twain is best known for his classic novels *The Adventures of Tom Sawyer* and *Adventures of Huckleberry Finn*, which are regarded as some of the greatest works of American literature.

2. **Jonathan Swift** (1667-1745) was an Irish writer, satirist, and clergyman, best known for his works of satire, such as *Gulliver's Travels* (1726) and "A Modest Proposal" (1729). In "A Modest Proposal", Swift suggests a rather shocking and absurd solution to poverty in Ireland by proposing that the impoverished Irish people should sell their children as food to the wealthy. It's a classic piece of satire that uses irony and exaggeration to criticize social and political issues of the time.

3. **Li Min** started working at *China Daily* as an art editor in 2010. She is in charge of illustrations for the homepages of the *China Daily European*, *China Daily*, etc. The cartoon is available at http://www.chinadaily.com.cn/opinion/cartoon/2015-06/13/content_20992588.htm.

4. **Luo Jie** (1968-) started working at *China Daily* in 2002. Now, he is deputy chief of the Art Department at *China Daily* and draws cartoons for the comments page. The cartoon is available at https://www.pinterest.com/pin/415949715587885753/.
5. **Phil Hands** is the editorial cartoonist for the Wisconsin State Journal in Madison, Wisconsin. The cartoon is available at https://journaltimes.com/opinion/cartoon/hands-on-wisconsin-sunshine-is-best-disinfectant-for-corruption/article_0b072169-9ef4-5036-b860-41abc87b3a8f.html.
6. **Matt Wuerker** (1956-) is a renowned American political cartoonist and founding staff member of *Politico*. Wuerker has received numerous accolades throughout his career, including the Pulitzer Prize for Editorial Cartooning in 2012. The cartoon is available at https://www.politico.com/cartoons/2024/03/04/matt-wuerker-cartoons-march-2024-00144716?slide=3.

Text A   Antony's Funeral Oration (Excerpt)

Preparatory Work

Activity 1 Who Are They?

Here is a list of some characters in the play Julius Caesar *by Shakespeare[1]. Who are they and what is the relationship between them?*

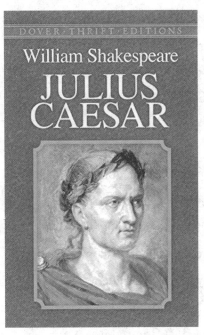

(Source: https://www.goodreads.com/book/show/13006.Julius_Caesar)

Extensive Reading 4

Characters	Who Are They?
Caesar	
Antony	
Brutus	
Cassius	
Calpurnia	
Portia	
Octavius	

Activity 2 Why Is Caesar Assassinated?

Act III, Scene I of Julius Caesar *is the pivotal scene where Caesar is assassinated by the conspirators. At the beginning of Act III, Scene II, Brutus first addresses the people to explain why they assassinated Caesar. How does he justify it? Identify the reasons from the following excerpt.*

BRUTUS:

    Be patient till the last.

    Romans, countrymen, and lovers! hear me for my

    cause, and be silent, that you may hear: believe me

    for mine honour, and have respect to mine honour,

    that you may believe: censure me in your wisdom,   5

    and awake your senses, that you may the better

    judge. If there be any in this assembly, any dear

    friend of Caesar's, to him I say that Brutus' love

    to Caesar was no less than his. If then that friend

demand why Brutus rose against Caesar, this is my answer: not that I loved Caesar less, but that I loved Rome more. Had you rather Caesar were living, and die all slaves, than that Caesar were dead, to live all free men? As Caesar loved me, I weep for him; as he was fortunate, I rejoice at it; as he was valiant, I honour him; but as he was ambitious, I slew him. There is tears for his love; joy for his fortune; honour for his valour; and death for his ambition. Who is here so base that would be a bondman? If any, speak; for him have I offended. Who is here so rude that would not be a Roman? If any, speak; for him have I offended. Who is here so vile that will not love his country? If any, speak; for him have I offended. I pause for a reply.

(Source: https://onlinecoursesblog.hillsdale.edu/the-assassination-of-julius-caesar/)

Extensive Reading 4

Reading the Text

Antony's Funeral Oration is commonly known as one of the most powerful and influential scenes in *Julius Caesar*. This pivotal moment occurs following the assassination of Julius Caesar, as his loyal friend Mark Antony steps forward to address the Roman crowd gathered for Caesar's funeral. With his skillful use of rhetoric, Antony masterfully manipulates the crowd's sentiment, turning them against the conspirators who orchestrated Caesar's death.

Antony's Funeral Oration
(Excerpt)
William Shakespeare

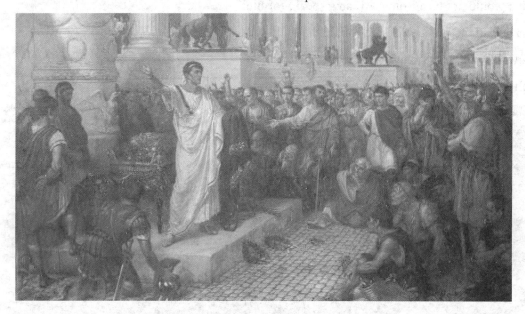

(Source: https://tikvahfund.org/tikvah-online/mark-antonys-funeral-oration-in-shakespeares-julius-caesar/)

Antony

    Friends, Romans, countrymen, lend me your ears;

    I come to bury Caesar, not to praise him;

    The evil that men do lives after them,

    The good is oft[2] interred with their bones,

    So let it be with Caesar… The noble Brutus   5

    Hath[3] told you Caesar was ambitious:

    If it were so, it was a grievous fault,

    And grievously hath Caesar answered it…

Here, under leave[4] of Brutus and the rest,

(For Brutus is an honourable man; 10

So are they all; all honourable men)

Come I to speak in Caesar's funeral….

He was my friend, faithful and just to me:

But Brutus says he was ambitious;

And Brutus is an honourable man…. 15

He hath brought many captives home to Rome,

Whose ransoms did the general coffers fill:

Did this in Caesar seem ambitious?

When that the poor have cried, Caesar hath wept:

Ambition should be made of sterner stuff: 20

Yet Brutus says he was ambitious;

And Brutus is an honourable man.

You all did see that on the Lupercal[5]

I thrice[6] presented him a kingly crown,

Which he did thrice refuse: was this ambition? 25

Yet Brutus says he was ambitious;

And, sure, he is an honourable man.

I speak not to disprove what Brutus spoke,

But here I am to speak what I do know.

You all did love him once, not without cause: 30

What cause withholds you then to mourn for him?

O judgment! thou art[7] fled to brutish beasts,

And men have lost their reason…. Bear with me;

My heart is in the coffin there with Caesar,

And I must pause till it come back to me. *[he weeps* 35

First Plebeian

Methinks[8] there is much reason in his sayings.

Second Plebeian

If thou consider rightly of the matter,

Caesar has had great wrong.

Third Plebeian

    Has he, masters?

    I fear there will a worse come in his place.   40

Fourth Plebeian

    Marked ye[9] his words? He would not take the crown;

    Therefore 'tis certain he was not ambitious.

First Plebeian

    If it be found so, some will dear abide it.

Second Plebeian

    Poor soul! his eyes are red as fire with weeping.

Third Plebeian

    There's not a nobler man in Rome than Antony.   45

Fourth Plebeian

    Now mark him, he begins again to speak.

Antony

    But yesterday the word of Caesar might

    Have stood against the world: now lies he there,

    And none so poor to do him reverence.

    O masters, if I were disposed to stir   50

    Your hearts and minds to mutiny and rage,

    I should do Brutus wrong, and Cassius wrong,

    Who, you all know, are honourable men:

    I will not do them wrong; I rather choose

    To wrong the dead, to wrong myself and you,   55

    Than I will wrong such honourable men.

    But here's a parchment with the seal of Caesar;

    I found it in his closet; 'tis his will:

    Let but the commons hear this testament—

    Which, pardon me, I do not mean to read—   60

    And they would go and kiss dead Caesar's wounds,

    And dip their napkins in his sacred blood,

    Yea, beg a hair of him for memory,

    And, dying, mention it within their wills,

>
> Bequeathing it as a rich legacy 65
> Unto their issue[10].

Fourth Plebeian

> We'll hear the will: read it, Mark Antony.

All

> The will, the will! we will hear Caesar's will!

Antony

> Have patience, gentle friends, I must not read it;
> It is not meet[11] you know how Caesar loved you. 70
> You are not wood, you are not stones, but men;
> And, being men, hearing the will of Caesar,
> It will inflame you, it will make you mad:
> 'Tis good you know not that you are his heirs;
> For if you should, O, what would come of it! 75

Fourth Plebeian

> Read the will; we'll hear it, Antony;
> You shall read us the will, Caesar's will.

Antony

> Will you be patient? will you stay awhile?
> I have o'ershot myself[12] to tell you of it:
> I fear I wrong the honourable men 80
> Whose daggers have stabbed Caesar; I do fear it.

Fourth Plebeian

> They were traitors: honourable men!

All

> The will! the testament!

Second Plebeian

> They were villains, murderers: the will! read the will!

Antony

> You will compel me then to read the will? 85
> Then make a ring about the corpse of Caesar,
> And let me show you him that made the will.
> Shall I descend? and will you give me leave?

Extensive Reading 4

All

    Come down.

Second Plebeian

    Descend.   *[Antony comes down*   90

Third Plebeian

    You shall have leave.

Fourth Plebeian

    A ring; stand round.

First Plebeian

    Stand from the hearse, stand from the body.

Second Plebeian

    Room for Antony, most noble Antony.

Antony

    Nay, press not so upon me; stand far off.   95

Several Plebeians

    Stand back. Room! Bear back.

(Source://www.1st-art-gallery.com/Lionel-Noel-Royer/Vercingetorix-Throws-Down-His-Arms-At-The-Feet-Of-Julius-Caesar-1899.html)

Antony

    If you have tears, prepare to shed them now.

You all do know this mantle: I remember

The first time ever Caesar put it on;

'Twas on a summer's evening, in his tent, 100

That day he overcame the Nervii[13]:

Look, in this place ran Cassius' dagger through:

See what a rent the envious Casca made:

Through this, the well-beloved Brutus stabbed;

And as he plucked his cursed steel away, 105

Mark how the blood of Caesar followed it,

As rushing out of doors to be resolved

If Brutus so unkindly knocked, or no:

For Brutus, as you know, was Caesar's angel:

Judge, O you gods, how dearly Caesar loved him! 110

This was the most unkindest cut of all;

For when the noble Caesar saw him stab,

Ingratitude, more strong than traitors' arms,

Quite vanquished him: then burst his mighty heart;

And, in his mantle muffling up his face, 115

Even at the base of Pompey's statue[14]

(Source: https://en.wikipedia.org/wiki/The_Death_of_Julius_Caesar)

Extensive Reading 4

(Which all the while ran blood), great Caesar fell.

O, what a fall was there, my countrymen!

Then I, and you, and all of us fell down,

Whilst bloody Treason flourished over us. 120

O, now you weep, and I perceive you feel

The dint of pity: these are gracious drops.

Kind souls, what weep you when you but behold

Our Caesar's vesture wounded? Look you here,

Here is himself, marred, as you see, with traitors. 125

[he plucks off the mantle

First Plebeian

O piteous spectacle!

Second Plebeian

O noble Caesar!

Third Plebeian

O woeful day!

Fourth Plebeian

O traitors, villains!

First Plebeian

O most bloody sight! 130

Second Plebeian

We will be revenged.

All

Revenge! About! Seek! Burn! Fire! Kill! Slay!

Let not a traitor live!

Antony

Stay, countrymen.

First Plebeian

Peace there! hear the noble Antony. 135

Second Plebeian

We'll hear him, we'll follow him, we'll die with him.

Antony

Good friends, sweet friends, let me not stir you up

To such a sudden flood of mutiny:

They that have done this deed are honourable.

What private griefs they have, alas, I know not,   140

That made them do it: they are wise and honourable,

And will, no doubt with reasons answer you.

I come not, friends, to steal away your hearts:

I am no orator, as Brutus is;

But, as you know me all, a plain blunt man,   145

That love my friend; and that they know full well

That gave me public leave to speak of him:

For I have neither wit, nor words, nor worth,

Action, nor utterance, nor the power of speech

To stir men's blood: I only speak right on;   150

I tell you that which you yourselves do know;

Show you sweet Caesar's wounds, poor poor dumb mouths[15],

And bid them speak for me: but were I Brutus,

And Brutus Antony, there were an Antony

Would ruffle up your spirits, and put a tongue   155

In every wound of Caesar, that should move

The stones of Rome to rise and mutiny.

All

We'll mutiny.

First Plebeian

We'll burn the house of Brutus.

Third Plebeian

Away, then! come, seek the conspirators.   160

Antony

Yet hear me, countrymen; yet hear me speak.

All

Peace, ho! Hear Antony! Most noble Antony!

Antony

Why, friends, you go to do you know not what:

Wherein[16] hath Caesar thus deserved your loves?

　　　　Alas, you know not; I must tell you then: 165

　　　　You have forgot the will I told you of.

All

　　　　Most true: the will! Let's stay and hear the will.

Antony

　　　　Here is the will, and under Caesar's seal.

　　　　To every Roman citizen he gives,

　　　　To every several[17] man, seventy-five drachmas. 170

Second Plebeian

　　　　Most noble Caesar! we'll revenge his death.

Third Plebeian

　　　　O royal Caesar!

Antony

　　　　Hear me with patience.

All

　　　　Peace, ho!

Antony

　　　　Moreover, he hath left you all his walks, 175

　　　　His private arbours and new-planted orchards,

　　　　On this side Tiber[18]; he hath left them you,

　　　　And to your heirs for ever; common pleasures,

　　　　To walk abroad and recreate yourselves.

　　　　Here was a Caesar! when comes such another? 180

First Plebeian

　　　　Never, never. Come, away, away!

　　　　We'll burn his body in the holy place,

　　　　And with the brands fire the traitors' houses.

　　　　Take up the body.

Second Plebeian

　　　　Go fetch fire! 185

Third Plebeian

　　　　Pluck down benches!

Fourth Plebeian

Pluck down forms[19], windows, anything.

[they rush forth; the bearer follow with the body

Antony

Now let it work. Mischief, thou art afoot,

Take thou what course thou wilt[20].

(Source: The excerpts in the text are taken from Act III, Scene II of *Julius Caesar* published by Cambridge University Press in 2009.)

Notes

1. ***Julius Caesar* by Shakespeare,** which consists of five acts, is a historical tragedy that depicts the conspiracy against the mighty Roman ruler Julius Caesar, his assassination, and the aftermath of his death. Julius Caesar (100 BC-44 BC) was a prominent Roman statesman and military general who played a critical role in the demise of the Roman Republic and the rise of the Roman Empire.
2. **"oft"** is a contraction of "often". It is an archaic form of the word that was commonly used during Shakespeare's time.
3. **"Hath"** is an archaic form of "has" that was commonly used during the Early Modern English period.
4. **"under leave"** in this context means "with permission".
5. **The Lupercal** was an ancient Roman festival celebrated on February 15th in honor of Lupercus, the Roman god of fertility and agriculture.
6. **"thrice"** means "three times".
7. **"art"** in this context means "are".
8. **"Methinks"** is an old-fashioned way of saying "I think" or "it seems to me."
9. **"mark'd ye"** is an archaic form of "did you mark," where "mark" means "to pay close attention to" or "to take note of."
10. **"Issue"** in this context refers to one's children, heirs, or descendants.
11. **"meet"** in this context means "appropriate".
12. **"I have o'ershot myself"** means "I have gone further than I should."
13. **The Nervii** were a Belgic tribe that inhabited the region of present-day Belgium during ancient times. They were one of the most powerful and warlike tribes in the region and were known for their fierce resistance against Roman conquest.
14. **The Pompey statue** refers to the statue of Gnacus Pompeius Magnus (106BC-48 BC), commonly known as Pompey the Great, who was a prominent military and political leader in ancient Rome during the late Roman Republic era.

Extensive Reading 4

15. **"wounds...mouths"** was a common metaphor in medieval literature to compare gaping wounds to mouths. In this context, these mouths are mute, unable to utter words—until Antony "bid them speak for [him]."
16. **"wherein"** means "for what".
17. **"several"** means "individual".
18. **Tiber** refers to the Tiber River, which is a significant river in central Italy, flowing through the city of Rome.
19. **"forms"** means "benches".
20. **"Thou wilt"** is an archaic way of saying "you will" or "you choose." It indicates that the mischief will take whichever path or outcome it chooses.

Remembering and Understanding

Activity 1 Sequence the Main Events

Following Brutus's speech in Act III, Scene II, Antony is allowed to give a funeral oration for Caesar in the market place under the condition that he does not speak ill of the conspirators. Arrange the following statements in the right order according to what happens in Act III, Scene II.

1. Antony repeatedly refers to the conspirators as "honourable men", but his tone and the context reveal his true meaning, subtly undermining their credibility.
2. Antony's speech stirs the crowd into a murderous riot, demanding justice for Caesar's death and calling for the conspirators to be punished.
3. Antony also reads them Caesar's will, in which Caesar leaves public land and money to each Roman citizen.
4. After Brutus speaks, the crowd becomes calm and supports his cause.
5. Antony then addresses the crowd with the famous line, "Friends, Romans, countrymen, lend me your ears", and immediately captures their attention and establishes a connection with them.
6. Brutus explains the conspirators' reasons for killing Caesar, emphasizing that they acted out of love for Rome, and the preservation of its liberty.
7. Antony presents evidence to counter Brutus's claims that Caesar was ambitious.
8. Antony vividly describes Caesar's wounded body, and displays Caesar's bloodied mantle.
9. Antony presents Caesar's will, and hints at its content, but hesitates to read it, causing growing agitation among the crowd.

Activity 2 True or False Questions

Are the following statements true or false? Make your decisions based on the text.

(   ) 1. Antony justifies Caesar's actions by highlighting Caesar's love and care for the people.

(   ) 2. Antony believes that the conspirators who killed Caesar are honourable.

(   ) 3. The plebeians initially doubt Antony's words and do not sympathize with him.

(   ) 4. Antony believes that revealing Caesar's will would not incite the crowd's emotions.

(   ) 5. The plebeians weep and feel pity when Antony shows them Caesar's wounded mantle.

(   ) 6. Caesar was killed in his tent by Cassius' dagger.

(   ) 7. The unkindest cut of all was when Brutus stabbed Caesar.

(   ) 8. Antony claims that he is a skilled orator like Brutus.

(   ) 9. Antony reveals that Caesar left his walks, arbors, and orchards to the Roman citizens.

(   ) 10. The plebeians decide to burn Brutus's body in a holy place.

Reasoning and Analyzing

Activity 1 Analyze Rational Appeals

In his speech, Brutus indicates that the assassination is out of concern for the general welfare of Rome because Caesar was ambitious and would become a tyrant. How does Antony undermine his justification? Fill in the table with missing information.

Evidence Against Brutus's Claim That Caesar Was Ambitious	Reasoning
1. He hath brought many captives home to Rome, Whose ransoms did the general coffers fill.	Antony questions whether bringing captives back to Rome for the benefit of the state can be considered an act of ambition, highlighting Caesar's contributions to Rome's wealth and well-being.
2.	
3.	
4.	

Extensive Reading 4

Activity 2 Answer the Following Questions

1. Why do you think Antony chooses to start his speech by repeatedly calling Brutus and the conspirators "honourable men"? What effect does this repetition have on the crowd's perception?
   _____
   _____

2. Based on Antony's depiction of Caesar's wounds and the bloody mantle, what emotions do you infer he is trying to evoke in the plebeians? How does this contribute to his overall argument?
   _____
   _____

3. When Antony displays Caesar's will to the crowd, what can you infer about the content of the will and its impact on the plebeians' sentiments towards Caesar and the conspirators?
   _____
   _____

4. How does Antony's mention of Caesar's acts of generosity and compassion towards the Roman citizens help in shaping the crowd's perception of Caesar's character? What emotional response does Antony aim to evoke through these examples?
   _____
   _____

5. In what ways does Antony indirectly criticize the conspirators' justification for Caesar's assassination? How does he use these devices to cast doubt on their motives and integrity?
   _____
   _____

Reflecting and Creating

Compare and Contrast

In Brutus's address, he claims that Caesar was ambitious while later Antony refutes that his claim is unfounded. Make a comparative study of the two speeches based on the following aspects:

❖ Central argument and main points made by each speaker

❖ Rational appeals used by each speaker

❖ Nonrational appeals used by each speaker

Aspects	Brutus's Address	Antony's Oration
Purpose		

Unit 5 Nonrational Appeals

(continued)

Aspects	Brutus's Address	Antony's Oration
Rational Appeals		
Nonrational Appeals		

Then have a discussion about the following questions:

❖ Which speaker do you find more effective in swaying the crowd? Why?

❖ What do you think of the nonrational appeals in Antony's oration? Are they legitimate or fallacious?

Text B Animal Rights V. Animal Research: A Modest Proposal

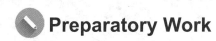 Preparatory Work

Here are some statements related to animal rights and animal research. Do you agree or disagree with them?

(Source: https://www.news-medical.net/health/Human-Health-Solutions-through-Animal-Research.aspx)

Statements	Agree	Disagree
1. Animal research is necessary for scientific advancements and medical breakthroughs.		

Extensive Reading 4

(continued)

Statements	Agree	Disagree
2. Animals have the same rights as humans and should not be used for any form of experimentation.		
3. It is ethical to use animals in research as long as it benefits human health and well-being.		
4. Animals have the ability to feel pain and suffering, and their welfare should be prioritized over scientific progress.		
5. Animals used in research should be treated humanely and have their pain minimized.		
6. The use of animals in cosmetic testing is unacceptable and should be banned worldwide.		
7. Researchers should be required to provide detailed justification for using animals in their studies.		
8. Animals used in research should be provided with the best possible living conditions and care.		
9. Animals have a lower moral status than humans, justifying their use in research.		
10. Animal rights activists play a vital role in raising awareness about the ethical treatment of animals in research.		
11. Animal rights activists often go to extremes and hinder scientific progress.		
12. Striking a balance between scientific progress and animal welfare is essential when considering the use of animals in research.		

Reading the Text

Using animals in research and to test the safety of products has been a topic of heated debate for decades. Opponents argue that animal research is unethical and inhumane, as it involves the suffering and exploitation of sentient beings. On the contrary, supporters believe that the benefits of such research, such as finding cures for diseases and improving human health, outweigh the ethical concerns. How does Bernstein tackle this contentious issue by drawing inspiration from Jonathan Swift's "A Modest Proposal"?

Animal Rights V. Animal Research:
A Modest Proposal[1]
Joseph Bernstein[2]

1   Many people love animals. Some animal lovers, though, in the name of their love, oppose the use of any animals in any medical research, regardless of the care given, regardless of the cause. Of course, many other animal lovers acknowledge the need for animal subjects in some medical studies, as long as no alternatives exist, and provided that care, respect and dignity are applied at all times. Unhappily, between the opponents of animal research and the researchers themselves lies no common ground, no place for an agreement to disagree: the opponents are not satisfied merely to abstain from animal experimentation themselves—they want everyone else to stop too.

(Source: https://ethicsandsociety.org/2018/01/12/whose-rights-are-right-the-debate-over-animal-rights-in-research/)

2   Despite that, I would argue that in this case (to a far greater extent than, say, in the case of abortion) the animal rights question can be answered by exactly that tactic: the abstention of the opposition. Of course, I do not advocate abstention from debate; and, of course, abstention from performing research by those who are not researchers is not meaningful. Rather, I propose that the protesters—and every citizen they can enlist—abstain from the benefits of animal research. Let them place fair market-place pressure on ending activities they find reprehensible. Let them mobilise the tacit support they claim. Let the market for therapies derived from animal research evaporate, and with it much of the funding for such work. Let the animal lovers attain their desired goal without clamour, and without violence.

3   To assist them, I offer a modest proposal.

Extensive Reading 4

4   I suggest that we adopt a legal release form, readily available to all patients, which will enable them to indicate precisely which benefits of animal research they oppose—and from which, accordingly, they refuse to benefit. This form could be sent to all hospitals and physicians, and would be included in the patient's chart, much like operative consent forms, or Do Not Resuscitate[3] instruction. It should resolve the issue once and for all.

5   This "Animal Research Advance Directive"[4] would look something like this:

6   Dear Doctor:

Animals deserve the basic freedom from serving as experiment subjects against their will. Today, we who are committed to seeing the world's scientific laboratories free from unwilling and innocent animals, hereby refuse to benefit from research performed on these victims.

(Source:https://www.animalaid.org.uk/the-issues/our-campaigns/animal-experiments/)

7   Accordingly, I ask that you care for me to the best of your abilities, but request that: (CHECK ALL THAT APPLY)

8   ☐ You do not perform on me a coronary bypass operation, or fix any heart defect my child may be born with, as these operations and the heart lung machine used during the procedures were developed using dogs. In fact, since the entire field of cardiology had been polluted by animal research for nearly a century, I cannot in good conscience accept any cardiological care.

9   ☐ You treat my child for any disease she may develop, but do not give her a vaccine that was tried first on a blameless animal. As I am not aware of any vaccines that were not animal-tested, please skip them all.

10   ☐ You avoid offering any suggestions regarding my diet and habits, when that information was derived from animal studies. This includes salt and fat intake, tobacco smoke, and various cancer-causing food additives. Do not bother to test my cholesterol level, as the association between high cholesterol and heart disease is knowledge stolen from the suffering of the innocent.

11   ☐ Should I develop a malignancy, you do not give me chemotherapy, as those drugs were administered

first to animals. I must also decline surgical treatment as well, since modern surgical technique and equipment owes its existence to sinful animal research. Finally, do not treat my disease with radiation, since that field, too, was contaminated by dog studies.

12 ☐ You amputate my leg or arm should I break it in such fashion that it requires surgery. Fracture fixation devices were designed through the suffering of dogs, so I must refuse repair of the bone. That probably will hurt a lot, but since I must refuse all pain medicine studied on rats (and that includes just about all of them), it is best if you just remove the damaged limb.

13 Needless to say, I will not accept an AIDS vaccine should one be developed, as unwilling Rhesus monkeys[5] have been used in AIDS research.

14 Thank you for considering my wishes. Only through the concerted avoidance of these ill-gotten technologies can we halt the barbaric practice of animal research. Of course, I have no objection to studying disease on humans. To that end, I pledge my body to science upon my death. It probably will occur a lot sooner than I'd like.

(Source: The article was published in the *Journal of Medical Ethics* in 1996.)

Notes

1. **Joseph Bernstein** is clinical professor of orthopaedic surgery at the University of Pennsylvania's hospital and a senior fellow at the Leonard Davis Institute of Health Economics, also at the University of Pennsylvania.
2. **"A Modest Proposal"** in the title is a nod to the satirical essay "A Modest Proposal" written by Jonathan Swift in 1729.
3. **Do Not Resuscitate** (DNR) instructions are medical orders that instruct healthcare providers not to perform cardiopulmonary resuscitation (CPR) in the event a person's heart or breathing stops.
4. **Animal Research Advance Directive** is a satirical term used by the author to describe a document that individuals could sign to indicate their refusal to benefit from any medical treatments or therapies that were developed through animal research. Advance Directive is a legal document (as a living will) signed by a competent person to provide guidance for medical and healthcare decisions (as the termination of life support or organ donation) in the event the person becomes incompetent to make such decisions.
5. **Rhesus monkeys** are a species of Old World monkeys known for their distinctive red faces and tails. They are native to South, Central, and Southeast Asia, and are widely used in scientific research due to their genetic and physiological similarities to humans.

Extensive Reading 4

Remembering and Understanding

Activity 1 Outline the Text

Fill in the blanks with appropriate words to get a structured outline of the text.

Outline

I. Introduction

❖ The divide between (1)_____

II. The proposal for (2)_____

❖ Abstaining from the (3)_____ of animal research

❖ Proposed outcomes of abstention

III. The modest proposal: the (4) "_____" form

❖ Purpose and implementation

❖ Refusing specific medical procedures or treatments (5) _____ animal research

IV. Examples of potential refusals

❖ Heart-related surgeries and treatments

❖ (6) _____

❖ (7) _____ suggestions and cholesterol levels tests

❖ Chemotherapy, surgery, and (8) _____ for cancer treatment

❖ (9) _____ and limb amputation

❖ Declining an AIDS vaccine

V. Conclusion

❖ Thanking for consideration of wishes

❖ (10) _____ body to science after death

Activity 2 Multiple-choice Questions

Choose the best answer to the question from the four choices given based on the text.

1. According to the essay, the central conflict between animal rights activists and researchers regarding animal experimentation is _____.

    A. the need for adequate care and respect for animals in research studies

    B. the lack of common ground and agreement to disagree between the two parties

    C. the ethical implications of using animals in medical research

    D. the desire of animal rights activists to stop all forms of animal experimentation

2. What tactic does Joseph Bernstein propose as a solution to the animal rights debate surrounding animal

research?

   A. Advocating for stricter regulations on animal experimentation.

   B. Encouraging dialogue and collaboration between animal lovers and researchers.

   C. Suggesting abstention from benefiting from therapies derived from animal research.

   D. Promoting alternative methods of medical research that do not involve animals.

3. The purpose of the "Animal Research Advance Directive" is _____.

   A. to provide guidelines for conducting ethical animal research studies

   B. to allow patients to specify which benefits of animal research they reject

   C. to promote the use of animals in medical research

   D. to address the issue of animal cruelty in scientific laboratories

4. According to the directive outlined in the essay, which of the following medical treatments would a patient reject if derived from animal research?

   A. Chemotherapy for malignancy.

   B. Dietary suggestions based on animal studies.

   C. AIDS vaccine developed using Rhesus monkeys.

   D. All of the above.

5. How does the essay conclude the proposal for the "Animal Research Advance Directive" and its potential impact?

   A. By emphasizing the importance of studying diseases on humans.

   B. By pledging the author's body to science upon their death.

   C. By suggesting that the practice of animal research can be halted through targeted abstention.

   D. By encouraging further debate and discussion on the ethical implications of animal research.

Reasoning and Analyzing

Activity 1 Answer the Following Questions

1. Do all animal lovers oppose animal research? How do the opponents of animal research differ from those who acknowledge its necessity?

   _____

   _____

2. What can be inferred from the use of "unhappily" in "Unhappily, between the opponents of animal research and the researchers themselves lies no common ground, no place for an agreement to disagree"(Para. 1)?

   _____

   _____

Extensive Reading 4

3. How does the suggested tactic to address the animal rights question, particularly in relation to animal research, differentiate itself from the case of abortion?

   _____
   _____

4. What is the underlying assumption regarding the market for therapies derived from animal research? How does the proposed tactic aim to allow the opponents to achieve their desired goal without resorting to clamour or violence?

   _____
   _____

5. Why does the author include such a long checklist in the "Animal Research Advance Directive"? What does he want to make clear to readers?

   _____
   _____

6. Does the author seriously expect to see the adoption of an "Animal Research Advance Directive"? Give your reasons please.

   _____
   _____

Activity 2 Analyze the Tone of the Text

"Animal Rights V. Animal Research: A Modest Proposal" is a nod to the satirical essay "A Modest Proposal" written by Jonathan Swift in 1729, in which Swift suggests a rather shocking and absurd solution to poverty in Ireland. What language and strategies help Bernstein create the satirical tone?

Language and Strategies	Examples
ridiculing language	"knowledge stolen from the suffering of the innocent"; "barbaric practice of animal research"

Reflecting and Creating

Topics for discussion and writing.

1. Satire is often used as a means of social commentary. What is your initial reaction to the essay's satirical tone? Do you think it effectively conveys the author's perspective on animal research and the opposition to it?

2. The author challenges the notion of selectively benefiting from medical advancements while opposing their origins in animal research. How do you navigate the ethical complexities of this issue in your own life? Are there instances where you find yourself conflicted or unsure about the use of animal-derived medical treatments?

3. The essay critiques the lack of common ground between opponents of animal research and researchers themselves. Can you think of potential ways to bridge this divide and foster a more constructive dialogue on the topic?

Summary

 Self-reflection

Fill out the checklist.

Area	Yes/No?	Notes/Comment
I know the common types of nonrational appeals.		
I know how to distinguish between rational and nonrational appeals.		
I know the role of nonrational appeals in arguments.		
I know the importance of using nonrational appeals legitimately in arguments.		
I have got a comprehensive understanding of both rational and nonrational appeals in Antony's oration in *Julius Caesar*.		
I can analyze and evaluate persuasive strategies used in creating the satirical tone in social commentary on controversial issues like animal rights v. animal research.		

Extensive Reading 4

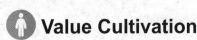

Value Cultivation

Activity 1 What Is Whole-process People's Democracy?

Here is a short excerpt about whole-process people's democracy taken from "Full Text of the Report to the 20th National Congress of the Communist Party of China". Read it and answer the following questions.

> China is a socialist country of people's democratic dictatorship under the leadership of the working class based on an alliance of workers and farmers; all power of the state in China belongs to the people. People's democracy is the lifeblood of socialism, and it is integral to our efforts to build a modern socialist country in all respects. Whole-process people's democracy is the defining feature of socialist democracy; it is democracy in its broadest, most genuine, and most effective form.
>
> We must firmly stay on the path of socialist political advancement with Chinese characteristics, uphold the unity between Party leadership, the running of the country by the people, and law-based governance, and ensure the principal position of the people, so as to give full expression to their will, protect their rights and interests, and spark their creativity.
>
> We will improve the system of institutions through which the people run the country. We will encourage the people's orderly participation in political affairs and guarantee their ability to engage in democratic elections, consultations, decision-making, management, and oversight in accordance with the law. We will inspire the people's motivation, initiative, and creativity, so as to consolidate and develop a lively, stable, and united political atmosphere.

1. According to the text, _____ is the defining feature of socialist democracy in China.

   A. party leadership and governance

   B. whole-process people's democracy

   C. law-based governance

   D unity between workers and farmers

2. What is the aim of encouraging the people's participation in political affairs, according to the text?

   A. Consolidating and developing a lively, stable, and united political atmosphere.

   B. Protecting the rights and interests of the people.

   C. Giving full expression to the will of the people.

   D. Sparking the creativity of the people.

Activity 2 Chinese Zodiac Culture

Europe has 12 constellations, while China has 12 animals symbolizing the 12 branches used to designate years. The 12 animals finish a cycle every 12 years and each of them guards one year. The 12 Chinese zodiac animals are in a fixed order:

Unit 5 Nonrational Appeals

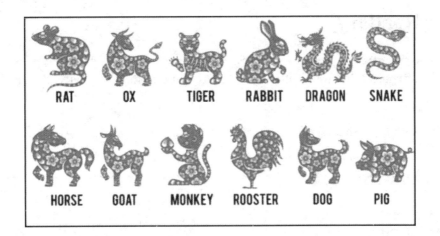

Chinese believe that those born in a certain year would inherit the traits of the animal guarding that year. For example, a Chinese horoscope may predict that a person born in the Year of the Horse would be, "cheerful, popular, and loves to compliment others". There are also many idioms of zodiac animals in Chinese culture. Identify the traits of each zodiac animal and translate the corresponding idiom into English.

Zodiac Animal	Traits	Idiom	English Translation
Rat		鼠目寸光	
Ox		庖丁解牛	
Tiger		如虎添翼	
Rabbit		守株待兔	
Dragon		龙飞凤舞	
Snake		杯弓蛇影	
Horse		一马当先	
Goat		亡羊补牢	
Monkey		猴年马月	
Rooster		闻鸡起舞	
Dog		白云苍狗	
Pig		猪突豨勇	

Extensive Reading 4

 Further Reading

1. "Full Text of the Report to the 20th National Congress of the Communist Party of China" by Xi Jinping （2022）
2. *Julius Caesar* by William Shakespeare (1601)
3. "A Reply to Joseph Bernstein" by Timothy Sprigge (1996)

Unit 6
Logical Fallacies

Mastering Critical Reading

We have thus far concentrated on the essential elements, patterns, and frameworks that enable people to argue rationally and forcefully, but it is undeniable that "arguments" that fail to meet the requirements of sound logic and robust reasoning are quite pervasive in our modern, media-centric world, frequently encountered both in our readings and daily interactions. Therefore, it is quite necessary for us to cultivate the ability to discern between well-reasoned and flawed arguments so as to reject conclusions that are either illogical or poorly substantiated. In this regard, a comprehensive study of argumentation must encompass an analysis of the cases when arguments go astray, which are more commonly referred to as logical fallacies.

■ **What Is a Logical Fallacy?**

A logical fallacy, or simply fallacy, is an error in reasoning that makes the argument seemingly sound or reasonable but actually flawed. While fallacious arguments often appear convincing, they fail to provide adequate support for the acceptance of their conclusions. Fallacies can manifest in any form of communication, ranging from casual conversations to scholarly writings, and they are often employed to mislead or divert attention from the truth, or to win the acceptance by appealing to emotions rather than reason.

People may commit logical fallacies unintentionally due to a variety of factors, such as insufficient or inaccurate knowledge on the subject, carelessness, attachment to their prejudices and bias, or the sheer complexity of the issue. However, it is not uncommon to find people resorting to fallacies intentionally, particularly when their objective is to manipulate others. Since fallacious arguments often appear reasonable although they are not, they can be used deliberately to trick those unguarded into acceptance.

■ **Some Common Fallacies**

The lists of fallacies can vary significantly in length among scholars, and the categorization of fallacies is equally diverse. But no matter how they are classified—into formal ones or informal ones, occurring in arguments or counterarguments, deriving from oversimplification or evasion of the real issue—the greatest importance lies in our alertness and capacity to detect fallacious reasoning so as to critically evaluate arguments and avoid being misled.

Sometimes we can identify the errors in reasoning solely by their form, which are commonly termed formal fallacies. A formal fallacy is a pattern of reasoning that is erroneous due to a flaw in the logical structure of the argument which renders the argument invalid. Such fallacies are "formal" because their flaws fall on the form or structure of the argument, rather than on its content. They can be identified and evaluated independently of the content of the argument. The following are two of the most common types of formal fallacies.

■ **Affirming the Consequent**

The fallacy of affirming the consequent looks like a typical form of deductive reasoning, but is invalid, hence fallacious.

Which of the following is a valid deductive reasoning, and which is fallacious?	
Example 1: If it is raining, then the ground is wet. It is raining. Therefore, the ground is wet.	**Example 2:** If it is raining, then the ground is wet. The ground is wet. Therefore, it is raining.

The fallacy of affirming the consequent takes the form "If P, then Q.// Q.// Therefore, P." It is fallacious because the premise only ensures the consequent Q from the antecedent P, but affirming the consequent fallacy goes the other way, arriving at antecedent P from consequent Q, which is not a guaranteed inference.

■ **Denying the Antecedent**

The fallacy of denying the antecedent follows the pattern "If P, then Q.// Not P.// Therefore, not Q." In this pattern, the premise establishes the consequent Q from the antecedent P, but this fallacy incorrectly infers the consequent of NOT Q from the negation of the antecedent, NOT P, which is by no means warranted from the premise.

What fallacies do the following examples commit?	
Example 1 If I am an English major, I have to study English. I am not an English major. Therefore, I will not study English.	**Example 2** If I am an English major, I have to study English. I'm now studying English. Therefore, I'm majoring in English.

Contrary to formal fallacies which focus on the form or structure of an argument, informal fallacies arise from the content of arguments in which the proposed conclusions are not supported by the premises. While formal fallacies can be spotted regardless of the subject matter, informal ones cannot be identified without a solid understanding of the content of the propositions. They take more varied forms and are more complex. The following is a short list of common informal fallacies that we are very likely to encounter or commit in arguments and everyday communication.

■ **Ad Hominem**

Ad hominem, a term from the Latin for "against the person", is a fallacy attempting to undermine an opponent's argument by attacking their personal characteristics, such as their appearance, character, education, or gender, instead of addressing the argument itself. The ad hominem attack is fallacious because, in most cases, a person's appearance, character, education, gender, or other personal traits are logically irrelevant to whether their proposition is true or false.

    Eg. You look too young and frivolous. There's just no way I can trust you to get this project done on time.

    Eg. Our female voters want better living conditions for domestic animals. Leave those sentimental women alone.

> **?** What is the problem with the above examples?

■ Bandwagon

The fallacy of bandwagon appeals to the popularity of an idea or action as the ground for its validity, suggesting that because many people think or do something, it must be correct. This fallacy presents what many people think or do with the intention to persuade the audience to think or perform in the same way. However, doing something because everyone else is doing it is not a logically valid reason for taking part in it.

    Eg. Of course it's fine to wait until the last minute to write your homework. Everybody does it!

    Eg. Smoking must be safe because millions of people have been doing it for years.

> **?** Is the appeal to popular opinion always fallacious? Why or why not?

■ False Dilemma

Also known as false dichotomy, either/or fallacy, black-or-white fallacy, the false dilemma fallacy presents two options or solutions as the only choices when more possibilities may exist. This kind of argument falsely limits the choices to just two options, one of which is usually unacceptable or unwanted obviously, and it totally ignores or dismisses the existence of alternative options.

    Eg. You either embrace AI and automation, or you want to live in the Stone Age.

    Eg. If you're not putting in overtime, you're not committed to your job.

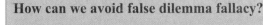

?	How can we avoid false dilemma fallacy?

■ **Loaded Question**

A loaded question is a trick question that presupposes one or more unverified assumptions that would unfairly influence the answer.

Eg. Are you still a heavy smoker?

Whether the person answers yes or no, the person is presupposed to have been a heavy smoker, no matter if it is true or not.

Eg. Are you finally ready to take your study seriously?

?	What is the problem with the second example? In which circumstance may it not be fallacious?

■ **Red Herring**

The red herring fallacy introduces an irrelevant topic in an attempt to mislead or distract the audience from the real issue. In essence, it is a deceptive tactic to evade the real subject and divert attention away from the main point of discussion.

Eg. Person A: I think it's terrible that a game hunter killed Cecil the lion.

Person B: What about all the babies that are killed every day by abortion?

Eg. Person A: How come you fail again in your math exam?

Person B: But I'm the star player on the school football team.

■ **Slippery Slope**

The slippery slope fallacy asserts that a certain step or action will lead to a chain of events, resulting in an undesirable—or sometimes really favorable—outcome, so we should prohibit—or promote—the first step or action from the beginning. However, no evidence is provided to ensure the occurrence of such a chain reaction.

Eg. If we ban Hummers because they are bad for the environment, eventually the government will ban all cars, so we should not ban Hummers.

Eg. If the government starts taxing junk food, it will soon put taxes on all processed food until we're only allowed to eat what they deem healthy.

> **?** What slippery slope fallacies have you encountered or committed?

■ Straw Man

The straw man fallacy refers to the distortion of other's argument to make it easier to attack. The flaw in this fallacy lies in its failure to actually respond to the original argument, but rather changing the subject to address a more manageable argument. Usually by exaggerating or oversimplifying other's proposition, one can easily attack and beat a weak version of it. In essence, the arguer is "setting up a straw man" which can be knocked down easily.

Eg. Person A: "I think we should have more regulations on industrial pollution to protect the environment."

Person B: "Why do you want to shut down all industries and destroy jobs?"

Eg. You are reading classical literature? Why do you think modern books are trash?

■ Begging the Question

The fallacy of begging the question assumes the conclusion in its premises. In other words, it's a form of circular reasoning where the very thing to be proved is already presupposed to be true. There are two main types of begging the question.

In the first type, the premise is just the equivalent to or the restatement of the conclusion. It takes the form "P; therefore, P".

Eg. People who work harder should get paid more because they do more work.

Eg. This restaurant is popular because so many people like eating here.

The second type of begging the question involves "circular reasoning." It argues in a circle because the premise of the argument depends on its conclusion. Generally, it takes the form "P is true because Q; Q is true because P." In the end, the argument comes full circle, without actually proving anything.

Eg. Person A: God wrote the Bible.

Person B: How do you know?

Person A: Because it says so in the Bible, and what the Bible says is true.

Person B: How do you know what the Bible says is true?

Person A: Because God wrote the Bible.

It is important to remember that the fallacies discussed here are far from exhaustive. Errors in reasoning can take many forms and occur in various contexts. Therefore, what really counts is not to name specific fallacies but to recognize the defects that weaken reasoning, and thus to refute them in other's arguments and avoid them in our own.

Enhancing Your Critical Reading

Identify the fallacies that the following statements commit.

Statements	Fallacies
1. Sherlock Holmes: You have a limp, which your therapist believes is psychosomatic. John Watson: How do you know I have a therapist? Sherlock Holmes: You have a psychosomatic limp; of course you have a therapist.	
2. If you are not a communist, you must be a capitalist.	
3. If you are getting enough vitamin C, you will be feeling healthy. Whenever I see someone looking healthy, I know they must be getting enough vitamin C.	
4. Have you stopped cheating in exams?	
5. Whenever my phone is out of power, it will turn off. I've just had my phone fully charged. So it won't turn off.	
6. Abortion reduces our respect for life. If we allow that to happen, soon we will be tolerant of violent acts like murder, and finally of war. To prevent our world from turning into hell, we should make abortion illegal right now.	
7. Green Peace's strategies aren't effective because they are all dirty, lazy hippies.	
8. When asked his solutions to the rising unemployment rate, a politician replies, "I have been working incredibly hard since I entered office, and I think the citizens can see this."	
9. People who don't support the proposed state minimum wage increase hate the poor.	
10. Yoga is the best way to explore our inner self because more and more people believe that yoga helps us to get in touch with our true inner being.	

Extensive Reading 4

Text A Love Is a Fallacy

Preparatory Work

Activity 1 What Is Love?

(Source: https://wallpaperaccess.com/cute-love)

Love is a timeless and enduring topic in artistic expression, particularly in literature. Countless tales of love have transcended time to become classics in the literary field. What is the most captivating love story you have ever read or heard of? What factors make that love story more appealing than others? Are you expecting to have such a love experience for yourself?

Appealing Love Stories	Factors That Make Them Attractive

Activity 2 Love, Beauty, Goodness, and Happiness

In our text excerpted from Symposium, Agathon contends that Love is the happiest of all gods because he is supreme in beauty and goodness. What do you think of the interconnection of love, beauty, goodness, and happiness?

(Source: https://www.publicdomainpictures.net/en/free-download.php?image=cupid&id=239974)

 Reading the Text

Charles Lamb[1], as merry and enterprising a fellow as you will meet in a month of Sundays, unfettered the informal essay with his memorable *Old China* and *Dream's Children*. There follows an informal essay that ventures even beyond Lamb's frontier, indeed, "informal" may not be quite the right word to describe this essay; "limp" or "flaccid" or possibly "spongy" are perhaps more appropriate.

Vague though its category, it is without doubt an essay. It develops an argument; it cites instances; it reaches a conclusion. Could Carlyle[2] do more? Could Ruskin[3]?

Read, then, the following essay which undertakes to demonstrate that logic, far from being a dry, pedantic discipline, is a living, breathing thing, full of beauty, passion, and trauma.

Author's Note

Love Is a Fallacy
Max Shulman[4]

(Source: https://www.wallpaperflare.com/pink-heart-decoration-love-hearts-mood-background-widescreen-wallpaper-tpvmz/download/1920x1080)

Extensive Reading 4

1   Cool was I and logical. Keen, calculating, perspicacious, acute and astute—I was all of these. My brain was as powerful as a dynamo, as precise as a chemist's scales, as penetrating as a scalpel. And—think of it!—I was only eighteen.

2   It is not often that one so young has such a giant intellect. Take, for example, Petey Bellows, my roommate at the University of Minnesota. Same age, same background, but dumb as an ox. A nice enough young fellow, you understand, but nothing upstairs. Emotional type. Unstable. Impressionable. Worst of all, a faddist. Fads, I submit, are the very negation of reason. To be swept up in every new craze that comes along, to surrender yourself to idiocy just because everybody else is doing it—this, to me, is the acme of mindlessness. Not, however, to Petey.

3   One afternoon I found Petey lying on his bed with an expression of such distress on his face that I immediately diagnosed appendicitis. "Don't move," I said. "Don't take a laxative. I'll get a doctor."

4   "Raccoon," he mumbled thickly.

5   "Raccoon?" I said, pausing in my flight.

6   "I want a raccoon coat," he wailed.

7   I perceived that his trouble was not physical, but mental. "Why do you want a raccoon coat?"

8   "I should have known it," he cried, pounding his temples. "I should have known they'd come back when the Charleston came back. Like a fool I spent all my money for textbooks, and now I can't get a raccoon coat."

9   "Can you mean," I said incredulously, "that people are actually wearing raccoon coats again?"

10 "All the Big Men on Campus are wearing them. Where've you been?"

11 "In the library," I said, naming a place not frequented by Big Men on Campus.

12 He leaped from the bed and paced the room, "I've got to have a raccoon coat," he said passionately. "I've got to!"

13 "Petey, why? Look at it rationally. Raccoon coats are unsanitary. They shed. They smell bad. They weight too much. They're unsightly. They—"

14 "You don't understand," he interrupted impatiently. "It's the thing to do. Don't you want to be in the swim?"

15 "No," I said truthfully.

16 "Well, I do," he declared. "I'd give anything for a raccoon coat. Anything!"

17 My brain, that precision instrument, slipped into high gear. "Anything?" I asked, looking at him narrowly.

18 "Anything," he affirmed in ringing tones.

19 I stroked my chin thoughtfully. It so happened that I knew where to set my hands on a raccoon coat. My

father had had one in his undergraduate days; it lay now in a trunk in the attic back home. It also happened that Petey had something I wanted. He didn't have it exactly, but at least he had first rights on it. I refer to his girl, Polly Espy.

20   I had long coveted Polly Espy. Let me emphasize that my desire for this young woman was not emotional in nature. She was, to be sure, a girl who excited the emotions but I was not one to let my heart rule my head. I wanted Polly for a shrewdly calculated, entirely cerebral reason.

21   I was a freshman in law school. In a few years I would be out in practice. I was well aware of the importance of the right kind of wife in furthering a lawyer's career. The successful lawyers I had observed were, almost without exception, married to beautiful, gracious, intelligent women. With one omission, Polly fitted these specifications perfectly.

22   Beautiful she was. She was not yet of pin-up proportions but I felt sure that time would supply the lack. She already had the makings.

23   Gracious she was. By gracious I mean full of graces. She had an erectness of carriage, an ease of bearing, a poise that clearly indicated the best of breeding. At table her manners were exquisite. I had seen her at the Kozy Kampus Korner eating the specialty of the house—a sandwich that contained scraps of pot roast, gravy, chopped nuts, and a dipper of sauerkraut—without even getting her fingers moist.

24   Intelligent she was not. In fact, she veered in the opposite direction. But I believed that under my guidance she would smarten up. At any rate, it was worth a try. It is, after all, easier to make a beautiful dumb girl smart than to make an ugly smart girl beautiful.

25   "Petey," I said, "are you in love with Polly Espy?"

26   "I think she's a keen kid," he replied, "but I don't know if you'd call it love. Why?"

27   "Do you," I asked, "have any kind of formal arrangement with her? I mean are you going steady or anything like that?"

28   "No. We see each other quite a bit, but we both have other dates. Why?"

29   "Is there," I asked, "any other man for whom she has a particular fondness?"

30   "Not that I know of. Why?"

31   I nodded with satisfaction. "In other words, if you were out of the picture, the field would be open. Is that right?"

32   "I guess so. What are you getting at?"

33   "Nothing, nothing," I said innocently, and took my suitcase out of the closet.

34   "Where are you going?" asked Petey.

35   "Home for the weekend." I threw a few things into the bag.

36   "Listen," he said, clutching my arm eagerly, "while you're home, you couldn't get some money from

your old man, could you, and lend it to me so I can buy a raccoon coat?"

37 "I may do better than that," I said with a mysterious wink and closed my bag and left.

38 "Look," I said to Petey when I got back Monday morning. I threw open the suitcase and revealed the huge, hairy, gamy object that my father had worn in his Stutz Bearcat in 1925.

39 "Holy Toledo!" said Petey reverently. He plunged his hands into the raccoon coat and then his face. "Holy Toledo!" he repeated fifteen or twenty times.

40 "Would you like it?" I asked.

41 "Oh yes!" he cried, clutching the greasy pelt to him. Then a canny look came into his eyes. "What do you want for it?"

42 "Your girl," I said, mincing no words.

43 "Polly?" he said in a horrified whisper. "You want Polly?"

44 "That's right."

45 He flung the coat from him. "Never," he said stoutly.

46 I shrugged. "Okay. If you don't want to be in the swim, I guess it's your business."

47 I sat down in a chair and pretended to read a book, but out of the corner of my eye I kept watching Petey. He was a torn man. First he looked at the coat with the expression of a waif at a bakery window. Then he turned away and set his jaw resolutely. Then he looked back at the coat, with even more longing in his face. Then he turned away, but with not so much resolution this time. Back and forth his head swiveled, desire waxing, resolution waning. Finally he didn't turn away at all; he just stood and stared with mad lust at the coat.

48 "It isn't as though I was in love with Polly," he said thickly. "Or going steady or anything like that."

49 "That's right," I murmured.

50 "What's Polly to me, or me to Polly?"

51 "Not a thing," said I.

52 "It's just been a casual kick—just a few laughs, that's all."

53 "Try on the coat," said I.

54 He complied. The coat bunched high over his ears and dropped all the way down to his shoe tops. He looked like a mound of dead raccoons. "Fits fine," he said happily.

55 I rose from my chair. "Is it a deal?" I asked, extending my hand.

56 He swallowed. "It's a deal," he said and shook my hand.

57 I had my first date with Polly the following evening. This was in the nature of a survey; I wanted to find out just how much work I had to do to get her mind up to the standard I required. I took her first to dinner. "Gee, that was a delish dinner," she said as we left the restaurant. Then I took her to a movie. "Gee, that was

a marvy movie," she said as we left the theater. And then I took her home. "Gee, I had a sensaysh time," she said as she bade me good night.

58   I went back to my room with a heavy heart. I had gravely underestimated the size of my task. This girl's lack of information was terrifying. Nor would it be enough merely to supply her with information. First she had to be taught to *think*. This loomed as a project of no small dimensions, and at first I was tempted to give her back to Petey. But then I got to thinking about her abundant physical charms and about the way she entered a room and the way she handled a knife and fork, and I decided to make an effort.

59   I went about it, as in all things, systematically. I gave her a course in logic. It happened that I, as a law student, was taking a course in logic myself, so I had all the facts at my finger tips. "Polly," I said to her when I picked her up on our next date, "tonight we are going over to the Knoll and talk."

60   "Oo, terrif," she replied. One thing I will say for this girl: you would go far to find another so agreeable."

61   We went to the Knoll, the campus trysting place, and we sat down under an old oak, and she looked at me expectantly. "What are we going to talk about?" she asked.

62   "Logic."

63   She thought this over for a minute and decided she liked it. "Magnif," she said.

64   "Logic," I said, clearing my throat, "is the science of thinking. Before we can think correctly, we must first learn to recognize the common fallacies of logic. These we will take up tonight."

65   "Wow-dow!" she cried, clapping her hands delightedly.

66   I winced, but went bravely on. "First let us examine the fallacy called Dicto Simpliciter."

67   "By all means," she urged, batting her lashes eagerly.

68   "Dicto Simpliciter means an argument based on an unqualified generalization. For example: Exercise is good. Therefore everybody should exercise."

69   "I agree," said Polly earnestly. "I mean exercise is wonderful. I mean it builds the body and everything."

70   "Polly," I said gently, "the argument is a fallacy. *Exercise is good* is an unqualified generalization. For instance, if you have heart disease, exercise is bad, not good. Many people are ordered by their doctors not to exercise. You must *qualify* the generalization. You must say exercise is *usually* good, or exercise is good *for most people*. Otherwise you have committed a Dicto Simpliciter. Do you see?"

71   "No," she confessed. "But this is marvy. Do more! Do more!"

72   "It will be better if you stop tugging at my sleeve," I told her, and when she desisted, I continued: "Next we take up a fallacy called Hasty Generalization. Listen carefully: You can't speak French. I can't speak French. Petey Bellows can't speak French. I must therefore conclude that nobody at the University of Minnesota can speak French."

73 "Really?" said Polly, amazed. "*Nobody?*"

74 I hid my exasperation. "Polly, it's a fallacy. The generalization is reached too hastily. There are too few instances to support such a conclusion."

75 "Know any more fallacies?" she asked breathlessly. "This is more fun than dancing even."

76 I fought off a wave of despair. I was getting nowhere with this girl, absolutely nowhere. Still, I am nothing if not persistent. I continued. "Next comes Post Hoc. Listen to this: Let's not take Bill on our picnic. Every time we take him out with us, it rains."

77 "I know somebody like that," she exclaimed. "A girl back home—Eula Becker, her name is, it never falls. Every single time we take her on a picnic—"

78 "Polly," I said sharply, "it's a fallacy. Eula Becker doesn't cause the rain. She has no connection with the rain. You are guilty of Post Hoc if you blame Eula Becker."

79 "I'll never do that again," she promised contritely. "Are you mad at me?"

80 I sighed deeply. "No, Polly, I'm not mad."

81 "Then tell me some more fallacies."

82 "All right. Let's try Contradictory Premises."

83 "Yes, let's," she chirped, blinking her eyes happily.

84 I frowned, but plunged ahead. "Here's an example of Contradictory Premises: If God can do anything, can He make a stone so heavy that He won't be able to lift it?"

85 "Of course," she replied promptly.

86 "But if He can do anything, He can lift the stone," I pointed out.

87 "Yeah," she said thoughtfully. "Well, then I guess He can't make the stone."

88 "But He can do anything," I reminded her.

89 She scratched her pretty, empty head. "I'm all confused," she admitted.

90 "Of course you are. Because when the premises of an argument contradict each other, there can be no argument. If there is an irresistible force, there can be no immovable object. If there is an immovable object, there can be no irresistible force. Get it?"

91 "Tell me some more of this keen stuff," she said eagerly.

92 I consulted my watch. "I think we'd better call it a night. I'll take you home now, and you go over all the things you've learned. We'll have another session tomorrow night."

93 I deposited her at the girls' dormitory, where she assured me that she had had a perfectly terrific evening, and I went glumly to my room. Petey lay snoring in his bed, the raccoon coat huddled like a great hairy beast at his feet. For a moment I considered waking him and telling him that he could have his girl back. It seemed clear that my project was doomed to failure. The girl simply had a logic-proof head.

⁹⁴ But then I reconsidered. I had wasted one evening: I might as well waste another. Who knew? Maybe somewhere in the extinct crater of her mind, a few embers still smoldered. Maybe somehow I could fan them into flame. Admittedly it was not a prospect fraught with hope, but I decided to give it one more try.

⁹⁵ Seated under the oak the next evening I said, "Our first fallacy tonight is called Ad Misericordiam."

⁹⁶ She quivered with delight.

⁹⁷ "Listen closely," I said. "A man applies for a job. When the boss asks him what his qualifications are, he replies that he has a wife and six children at home, the wife is a helpless cripple, the children have nothing to eat, no clothes to wear, no shoes on their feet, there are no beds in the house, no coal in the cellar, and winter is coming."

⁹⁸ A tear rolled down each of Polly's pink cheeks. "Oh, this is awful, awful," she sobbed.

⁹⁹ "Yes, it's awful," I agreed, "but it's no argument. The man never answered the boss's questions about his qualifications. Instead he appealed to the boss's sympathy. He committed the fallacy of Ad Misericordiam. Do you understand?"

¹⁰⁰ "Have you got a handkerchief?" she blubbered.

¹⁰¹ I handed her a handkerchief and tried to keep from screaming while she wiped her eyes. "Next," I said in a carefully controlled tone, "we will discuss False Analogy. Here is an example: Students should be allowed to look at their textbooks during examinations. After all, surgeons have X-rays to guide them during an operation, lawyers have briefs to guide them during a trial, carpenters have blueprints to guide them when they are building a house. Why, then, shouldn't students be allowed to look at their textbooks during an examination?"

¹⁰² "There now," she said enthusiastically, "is the most marvy idea I've heard in years."

¹⁰³ "Polly," I said testily, "the argument is all wrong. Doctors, lawyers, and carpenters aren't taking a test to see how much they have learned, but students are. The situations are altogether different, and you can't make an analogy between them."

¹⁰⁴ "I still think it's a good idea," said Polly.

¹⁰⁵ "Nuts," I muttered. Doggedly I pressed on. "Next we'll try Hypothesis Contrary to Fact."

¹⁰⁶ "Sounds yummy," was Polly's reaction.

¹⁰⁷ "Listen: If Madame Curie had not happened to leave a photographic plate in a drawer with a chunk of pitchblende, the world today would not know about radium."

¹⁰⁸ "True, true," said Polly, nodding her head. "Did you see the movie? Oh, it just knocked me out. That Walter Pidgeon is so dreamy. I mean he fractures me."

¹⁰⁹ "If you can forget Mr. Pidgeon for a moment," I said coldly, "I would like to point out that the statement is a fallacy. Maybe Madame Curie would have discovered radium at some later date. Maybe somebody else would have discovered it. Maybe any number of things would have happened. You can't start with a

hypothesis that is not true and then draw any supportable conclusions from it."

110 "They ought to put Walter Pidgeon in more pictures," said Polly. "I hardly ever see him anymore."

111 One more chance, I decided. But just one more. There is a limit to what flesh and blood can bear. "The next fallacy is called Poisoning the Well."

112 "How cute!" she gurgled.

113 "Two men are having a debate. The first one gets up and says, 'My opponent is a notorious liar. You can't believe a word that he is going to say.' ... Now, Polly, think. Think hard. What's wrong?"

114 I watched her closely as she knit her creamy brow in concentration. Suddenly, _____
_____.
"_____," she said with indignation. "_____
_____
_____"

115 "_____" I cried exultantly. "_____
_____
_____"

116 "Pshaw" she murmured, blushing with pleasure.

117 "You see, my dear, these things aren't so hard. All you have to do is concentrate. Think—examine—evaluate. Come now, let's review everything we have learned."

118 "Fire away," she said with an airy wave of her hand.

119 Heartened by the knowledge that Polly was not altogether a cretin, I began a long, patient review of all I had told her. Over and over and over again I cited instances, pointed out flaws, kept hammering away without letup. It was like digging a tunnel. At first everything was work, sweat, and darkness. I had no idea when I would reach the light, or even *if* I would. But I persisted. I pounded and clawed and scraped, and finally I was rewarded. I saw a chink of light. And then the chink got bigger and the sun came pouring in and all was bright.

120 Five grueling nights this took, but it was worth it. I had made a logician out of Polly; I had taught her to think. My job was done. She was worthy of me at last. She was a fit wife for me, a proper hostess for my many mansions, a suitable mother for my well-heeled children.

121 It must not be thought that I was without love for this girl. Quite the contrary. Just as Pygmalion[5] loved the perfect woman he had fashioned, so I loved mine. I determined to acquaint her with my feeling at our very next meeting. The time had come to change our relationship from academic to romantic.

122 "Polly," I said when next we sat beneath our oak, "tonight we will not discuss fallacies."

123 "Aw, gee," she said, disappointed.

124 "My dear," I said, favoring her with a smile, "we have now spent five evenings together. We have gotten along splendidly. It is clear that we are well matched."

125 "(1) _____," said Polly brightly.

126 "I beg your pardon," said I.

127 "(1) _____," she repeated. "How can you say that we are well matched on the basis of only five dates?"

128 I chuckled with amusement. The dear child had learned her lessons well. "My dear," I said, patting her hand in a tolerant manner, "five dates is plenty. After all, you don't have to eat a whole cake to know it's good."

129 "(2) _____", said Polly promptly. "I'm not a cake. I'm a girl."

130 I chuckled with somewhat less amusement. The dear child had learned her lessons perhaps too well. I decided to change tactics. Obviously the best approach was a simple, strong, direct declaration of love. I paused for a moment while my massive brain chose the proper words. Then I began:

131 "Polly, I love you. You are the whole world to me, and the moon and the stars and the constellations of outer space. Please, my darling, say that you will go steady with me, for if you will not, life will be meaningless. I will languish. I will refuse my meals. I will wander the face of the earth, a shambling, hollow-eyed hulk."

132 There, I thought, folding my arms, that ought to do it.

133 "(3) _____," said Polly.

134 I ground my teeth. I was not Pygmalion; I was Frankenstein[6], and my monster had me by the throat. Frantically I fought back the tide of panic surging through me. At all costs I had to keep cool.

135 "Well, Polly," I said, forcing a smile, "you certainly have learned your fallacies."

136 "You're darn right," she said with a vigorous nod.

137 "And who taught them to you, Polly?"

138 "You did."

139 "That's right. So you do owe me something, don't you, my dear? If I hadn't come along you never would have learned about fallacies."

140 "(4) _____," she said instantly.

141 I dashed perspiration from my brow. "Polly," I croaked, "you mustn't take all these things so literally. I mean this is just classroom stuff. You know that the things you learn in school don't have anything to do with life."

142 "(5) _____," she said, wagging her finger at me playfully.

143 That did it. I leaped to my feet, bellowing like a bull. "Will you or will you not go steady with me?"

144 "I will not," she replied.

Extensive Reading 4

145 "Why not?" I demanded.

146 "Because this afternoon I promised Petey Bellows that I would go steady with him."

147 I reeled back, overcome with the infamy of it. After he promised, after he made a deal, after he shook my hand! "The rat!" I shrieked, kicking up great chunks of turf. "You can't go with him, Polly. He's a liar. He's a cheat. He's a rat."

148 "(6) _____," said Polly, "and stop shouting. I think shouting must be a fallacy too."

149 With an immense effort of will, I modulated my voice. "All right," I said. "You're a logician. Let's look at this thing logically. How could you choose Petey Bellows over me? Look at me–a brilliant student, a tremendous intellectual, a man with an assured future. Look at Petey–a knot-head, a jitterbug, a guy who'll never know where his next meal is coming from. Can you give me one logical reason why you should go stead with Petey Bellows?"

150 "I certainly can," declared Polly. "He's got a raccoon coat."

(Source: This text is taken from *The Many Loves of Dobie Gillis* by Max Shulman.)

Notes

1. **Charles Lamb** (1775-1834) was an English essayist, poet, and critic of the English Romantic period, best known for his collections *Essays of Elia* (1823), *The Last Essays of Elia* (1833), and for the children's book *Tales from Shakespeare* (1807) which was co-authored with his sister Mary Lamb.
2. **Thomas Carlyle** (1795-1881) was a Scottish essayist, satirist, and historian, whose major works include *Sartor Resartus* (1836), *The French Revolution*, 3 vol. (1837), *On Heroes, Hero-Worship, and the Heroic in History* (1841), *Oliver Cromwell's Letters and Speeches: With Elucidation* (1845), and *History of Friedrich II of Prussia* (1858).
3. **John Ruskin** (1819-1900) was an English writer, art critic, art historian, painter, and polymath of the Victorian era. He was a prolific writer and his writing covers a vast range from art history to geology, architecture, myth, ornithology, literature, education, botany and political economy.
4. **Max Shulman** (1919-1988) was an American writer and humorist, best known for his mastery of satire. His first novel, *Barefoot Boy with Cheek* (1943), became a best seller and was regarded as a classic of campus humor. His following works enjoyed huge popularity and success, many of which were adapted to screen, including *The Many Loves of Dobie Gillis* (1951), *Rally Round the Flag, Boys!* (1957), and a Broadway play *The Tender Trap* (1954). From 1954 to 1970, Shulman wrote a syndicated weekly column, "On Campus".
5. **Pygmalion** is a king and also a sculptor in Greek mythology. He makes an ivory statue of his ideal woman and then falls in love with his own creation, which he names Galatea. The goddess Venus brings the statue to life in answer to his prayer.

6. **Frankenstein** is the title character in Mary Wollstonecraft Shelley's Gothic horror novel *Frankenstein* (1818), which tells the story of the scientist Victor Frankenstein, who brings to life a monstrous body from pieces of corpses out of his obsession with the secret of life. After being rejected by society, the monster turns upon its creator and eventually destroys him. The name Frankenstein has been popularly attached to the monster itself.

Remembering and Understanding

Activity 1 What's Wrong?

The last fallacy Polly learned is poisoning the well, and the protagonist offers an example before explaining it to Polly. Can you make out what is wrong in the example? Do you think Polly can identify the problem with the case? What clues from the text lead you to your conclusion? Design the answer from Polly and the response from the protagonist, and fill in the blanks in Paras. 114 and 115.

What's wrong in the example?
Do you think Polly can identify the problem with the case? What are the clues?
Fill in the blanks in Paras. 114 and 115.   114. I watched her closely as she knit her creamy brow in concentration. Suddenly, _____ _____."_____," she said with indignation. "_____ _____"   115. "_____" I cried exultantly. "_____ _____"

Extensive Reading 4

Activity 2 Identify the Fallacies

In the story, the protagonist teaches Polly altogether eight fallacies. Have you mastered these fallacies? Give a brief explanation and one more example of each fallacy.

Fallacy	Explanation	Example
Dicto Simpliciter		
Hasty Generalization		
Post Hoc		
Contradictory Premises		
Ad Misericordiam		
False Analogy		
Hypothesis Contrary to Fact		
Poisoning the Well		

Now identify the fallacies in the later part of the story and fill in the numbered blanks in the text.

Blank (1)	
Blank (2)	
Blank (3)	
Blank (4)	
Blank (5)	
Blank (6)	

Activity 3 Retell the Story

Who are the characters in the story? What initiates the major event? How does the plot develop? How does it end? Try to retell the story in your own words.

_____
_____
_____
_____
_____
_____
_____
_____

Reasoning and Analyzing

Answer the following questions.

1. What kind of person is the protagonist? What are the clues from the text?

   _____
   _____

2. Is Polly a smart girl? Why?

   _____
   _____

3. What kind of person is Petey Bellows as described by the protagonist? Is he really so? Why?

   _____
   _____

4. What are the features of the author's choice of words and sentences? What are the functions or effects of such language design?

   _____
   _____

5. What rhetorical devices does the author use in the text? What effects do they achieve?

   _____
   _____

Extensive Reading 4

6. The author, Max Shulman, was an American writer and humorist best known for his mastery of satire. Do you think this story is humorous and satirical? If so, where comes the humorous effect and of whom or of what is it satirical? If not, what is the stylistic feature of this story? Why?
   _____
   _____

7. What is the writing purpose of this story?
   _____
   _____

8. What does the author intend to mean by the title, "Love Is a Fallacy"? Is love a kind of fallacy like what we have learned in this unit?
   _____
   _____

Reflecting and Creating

Activity 1 Topics for Discussion and Writing

1. In love, some people may be blind, while some calculating. What do you think of these two inclinations in love? Is it necessary, and possible, to keep sensible in love?
2. In traditional Chinese culture, people are expected to marry a well-matched person in class, social status, economic situation, etc. Do you think it is reasonable to take these factors into consideration in marriage?
3. With this humorous love story, the author demonstrates that logic can be beautiful and lively. What is your previous impression of logic? Has it changed after you read this story? What is your impression of logic now? Is it beautiful and lively?
4. We have learned the fallacy of ad hominem at the beginning of this unit and the fallacy of poisoning the well in Text A. Is there any similarity between them? Where lies the difference? Search for more information on these two fallacies and present a comparison of them.

Activity 2 Detect Fallacies in Life

Logical fallacies, as shown in this story, are everywhere in our lives. Paying due attention, you can easily find many in your reading or real life. Collect 2 to 3 cases of logical fallacies in your life and share them in class. Try to see whether you can identify the fallacies in the examples from your classmates.

Notice that of a large amount of logical fallacies, we have only learned very few of them. So what really matters is that you can detect the fallacious reasoning in other's speaking or writing, not naming the exact types of the fallacies.

Text B The Devious Art of Lying by Telling the Truth

 Preparatory Work

Strictly speaking, we all tell lies often. For example, you might tell your parents your life recently is filled with joy and pleasure when you are actually overwhelmed by the stress of impending exams and feel quite depressed. Such lies are often given to avoid hurting someone's feelings or to avoid trouble, and not with malicious intention. They are commonly referred to as white lies. What are some of the white lies that you have ever told?

(Source of picture: https://thecontextofthings.com/2016/12/28/tell-a-lie/)

While the intention behind white lies is often to be considerate and kind, are such lies truly justifiable and acceptable? How can we distinguish between white lies and vicious ones?

My White Lies	Are They Acceptable?	How to Distinguish?

Extensive Reading 4

Reading the Text

> While lying is generally regarded as deceptive and unacceptable, there are circumstances where telling the truth can be equally misleading. Lying by telling the truth, termed "paltering" by psychologists, is pervasive in our lives, but it is often difficult to detect and challenge it.

The Devious Art of Lying by Telling the Truth
Melissa Hogenboom[1]

1   It is no secret that politicians often lie, but consider this—they can do so simply by telling the truth. Confused?

2   That statement becomes clearer when you realise that we've probably all done it. A classic example might be if your mum asks if you've finished your homework and you respond: "I've written an essay on Tennessee Williams for my English class." This may be true, but it doesn't actually answer the question about whether your homework was done. That essay could have been written long ago and you have misled your poor mother with a truthful statement. You might not have even started your homework yet.

3   Misleading by "telling the truth" is so pervasive in daily life that a new term has recently been employed by psychologists to describe it: paltering. That it is so widespread in society now gives us more insight into the grey area between truth and lies, and perhaps even why we lie at all.

4   We lie all the time, despite the fact that it costs us considerably more mental effort to lie than to tell the truth. US president Abraham Lincoln once said that "no man has a good enough memory to be a successful liar".

5   In 1996 one researcher, Bella DePaulo even put a figure on it. She found that each of us lies about once or twice a day. She discovered this by asking participants for one week to note down each time they lied, even if they did so with a good intention. Out of the 147 participants in her original study, only seven said they didn't lie at all—and we can only guess if they were telling the truth.

6   Many of the lies were fairly innocent, or even kind, such as: "I told her that she looked good when I thought that she looked like a blimp." Some were to hide embarrassment, such as pretending a spouse had not been fired. DePaulo, a psychologist at the University of California Santa Barbara, says that the participants in her study were not aware of how many lies they told, partly because most were so "ordinary and so expected that we just don't notice them".

7   It is when individuals use lies to manipulate others or to purposely mislead that it is more worrying. And this happens more often than you might think.

8   When Todd Rogers and his colleagues were looking at how often politicians dodge questions during debates they realised something else was going on. By stating another truthful fact, they could get out of answering a question. They could even imply something was truthful when it was not. Politicians do this all the time, says Rogers, a behavioural scientist at Harvard Kennedy School. He and colleagues therefore set out to understand more about it.

9   He found that paltering was an extremely common tactic of negotiation. Over half the 184 business executives in his study admitted to using the tactic. The research also found that the person doing the paltering believed it was more ethical than lying outright.

10   The individuals who had been deceived, however, did not distinguish between lying and paltering. "It probably leads to too much paltering as communicators think that when disclosed, it will be somewhat ethical, whereas listeners see it as a lie," says Rogers.

11   It is also difficult to spot a misleading "fact" when we hear something that on the face of it, sounds true. For instance, the UK's Labour Party campaign video to lower the voting age said: "You're 16. Now you can get married, join the Army, work full-time." The BBC's reality check team discovered that these facts do not tell the whole truth.

12   "You can only join the Army aged 16 or 17 with your parents' permission," the Reality Check team wrote. "At that age you also need your parents' permission to get married unless you do so in Scotland. Since 2013, 16 and 17-year-olds cannot work full-time in England, but can in the other three home nations with some restrictions."

13   In another example, the then-presidential-nominee Donald Trump paltered during the presidential debates. He was questioned about a housing discrimination lawsuit early on in his career and stated that his company had given "no admission of guilt". While they may not have admitted it, an investigation by the New York Times found that his company did discriminate based on race.

14   And even if we do spot misleading truths, social norms can prevent us from challenging whether or not they are deceptive. Take a now infamous interview in the UK, where journalist Jeremy Paxman interviewed the politician Michael Howard (pictured below). He repeatedly asks Howard whether he "threatened to

Extensive Reading 4

overrule" the then prisons governor. Howard in turn, continues to evade the question with other facts in a bizarre exchange that becomes increasingly awkward to watch. Not many of us are comfortable challenging someone in that way.

15 While it's common in politics, so too is it in everyday life. Consider the estate agent who tells a potential buyer that an unpopular property has had "lots of enquiries" when asked how many actual bids there have been. Or the used car salesman who says a car started up extremely well on a frosty morning, without disclosing that it broke down the week before. Both statements are true but mask the reality of the unpopular property and the dodgy car.

16 Paltering is perhaps so commonplace because it is seen as a useful tool. It happens because we constantly have so many competing goals, suggests Rogers. "We want to achieve our narrow objective – [selling a house or car] – but we also want people to see us as ethical and honest." He says these two goals are in tension and by paltering, people believe they are being more ethical than outright lying. "We show evidence they are making a mistake," says Rogers.

17 We can see the problems this sort of thinking can cause reflected in society today. The public are clearly sick of being lied to and trust in politicians is plummeting. One 2016 poll found that the British public trust politicians less than estate agents, bankers and journalists.

18 And despite the fact that we now frequently expect lies from those in power, it remains challenging to spot them in real time, especially so if they lie by paltering. Psychologist Robert Feldman, author of The Liar in Your Life, sees this as worrying both on a personal and on a macro level. "When we're lied to by people in power, it ruins our confidence in political institutions – it makes the population very cynical about [their] real motivations."

19 Lying can and does clearly serve a devious social purpose. It can help someone paint a better picture than the truth, or help a politician dodge an uncomfortable question. "It's unethical and it makes our democracy worse. But it's how human cognition works," says Rogers.

20 Unfortunately, the prevalence of lies might stem from the way we are brought up. Lies play a role in our social interactions from a very young age. We tell young children about tooth fairies and Santa, or encourage a child to be grateful for an unwanted present. "We give our kids very mixed messages," says Feldman. "What they ultimately learn is that even though honesty is the best policy, it's also at times fine and preferable to lie about things."

21 So next time you hear a fact that sounds odd, or someone to be deflecting a question, be aware that what you think is the truth may very well be deceptive.

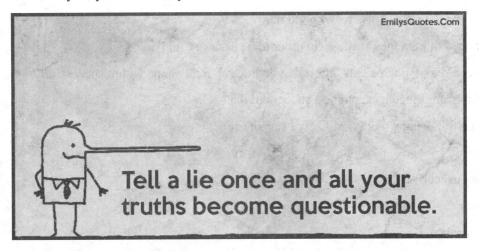

(Source: https://emilysquotes.com/tell-a-lie-once-and-all-your-truths-become-questionable/)

(Source: This article was published on *BBC* on November 15, 2017.)

Notes
1. Melissa Hogenboom is BBC Future's feature writer, a multi-award-winning filmmaker and a leader at the BBC where she launched and leads the documentary site BBC Reel.

✎ Remembering and Understanding

Choose the best answer to each question from the four choices given based on the text.

1. Which of the following lies is *least* likely to be accepted according to the author?

   A. You tell your friend she looks good when she does not.

   B. You tell your mom you have finished your homework when you haven't.

   C. An estate agent tells a potential buyer the house is favored by many when it is unpopular.

   D. A politician tells part of fact or irrelevant information to dodge a question or to mislead when the question is challenging.

Extensive Reading 4

2. What is paltering?

   A. It is misleading by telling the truth.

   B. It is lying.

   C. It is the grey area between truth and lies.

   D. It is the reason why we lie.

3. What does the author intend to mean by the quote from Abraham Lincoln in Para. 4— "no man has a good enough memory to be a successful liar"?

   A. None of the people can be a really good liar.

   B. People need to train their memory in order to be a successful liar.

   C. Lying requires so much mental effort that no one can really cope with it successfully.

   D. Even Abraham Lincoln cannot be a successful liar.

4. Which of the following would most likely use paltering?

   A. Politicians.

   B. Business executives.

   C. Salesmen.

   D. All of the above.

5. What's the problem with Donald Trump's answer of "no admission of guilt" in Para. 13 according to the text?

   A. He should not attend the debates.

   B. He did not answer the question of whether his company committed discrimination.

   C. His company did discriminate based on race.

   D. He was not polite in answering the question.

6. Why is paltering so commonly used?

   A. Because people intend to fulfill their competing goals while keeping ethical.

   B. Because paltering is more ethical since it is not lying.

   C. Because people are brought up in lies.

   D. Because paltering can bring people fame and profit.

Unit 6 Logical Fallacies

Reasoning and Analyzing

Answer the following questions.

1. What does the example in Para. 2 illustrate?

2. What is the possible limitation of Bella DePaulo's research? What might the author think of her research result?

3. What does the author think of lying?

4. What is the difference between Bella DePaulo's research and that by Todd Rogers and his colleagues?

5. Where lies the difficulty in fighting against paltering?

6. Why is paltering preferred as a useful tool by some people? Does the author think so?

7. What is the author's attitude towards paltering? What are the clues?

8. According to the author, how will stories about tooth fairies and Santa influence children? What is the author's attitude towards this influence?

Extensive Reading 4

 Reflecting and Creating

Topics for discussion and writing.

1. As the author acknowledges, some lies can be fairly innocent, or even kind. Similarly, sometimes we use euphemisms to be polite and kind. In which situations and for what purposes do people usually use euphemisms? What are the similarities and differences between using euphemisms and paltering?

2. While lying is always connected with being deceptive and problematic, is it ideal to tell the truth only? Is it even plausible? Why? When is it justified to tell lies?

3. One of the common fallacies, red herring, aims at misleading or distracting the audience with irrelevant topics. Consult more information on this fallacy, and make out the similarities and differences between red herring and paltering.

Summary

 Self-reflection

Fill out the checklist.

Area	Yes/No?	Notes/Comment
I know what a logical fallacy is.		
I know the distinction between formal fallacies and informal fallacies.		
I know the typical formal fallacies of affirming the consequent and denying the antecedent.		
I know the common informal fallacies of ad hominem, bandwagon, false dilemma, loaded question, red herring, slippery slope, strawman, and begging the question.		
I know the common fallacies of dicto simpliciter, hasty generalization, post hoc, contradictory premises, ad misericordiam, false analogy, hypothesis contrary to fact, and poisoning the well.		

Area	Yes/No?	Notes/Comment
I can detect some common fallacies in life.		
I have got a deeper understanding of love.		
I understand that telling the truth can be misleading and deceptive sometimes.		

(continued)

Value Cultivation

Activity 1 Love Stories in Western and Chinese Cultures

Do you know the story of Romeo and Juliet? You may search for information on this famous tragedy by William Shakespeare and give a brief recount of the story.

What story in Chinese culture bears a similar plot to that of Romeo and Juliet? Tell the story to the class.

The story of Romeo and Juliet	The Chinese story

In which way are the two stories similar? What are the differences between them?

Similarities	Differences

What are the major factors that lead to their tragedies respectively?

For the tragedy of Romeo and Juliet	For the tragedy in the Chinese story

Extensive Reading 4

Activity 2 The Best Match

Choose from the following quotes the one that matches the central idea of Text B best. _____

A. The most common lie is that which one lies to himself; lying to others is relatively an exception.

—Friedrich Nietzsche

B. Honesty is more than not lying. It is truth telling, truth speaking, truth living, and truth loving.

—James E. Faust

C. The essence of lying is in deception, not in words.　　　　　　　　　　—John Ruskin

D. Half a truth is often a great lie.　　　　　　　　　　　　　　　—Benjamin Franklin

E. The best liar is he who makes the smallest amount of lying go the longest way.　—Samuel Butler

F. If evil be spoken of you and it be true, correct yourself, if it be a lie, laugh at it.　—Epictetus

G. 天可度，地可量，唯有人心不可防。但见丹诚赤如血，谁知伪言巧似簧。

——《天可度·恶诈人也》[唐] 白居易

H. 志不强者智不达，言不信者行不果。　　　　——《墨子·修身》[春秋末战国初]

I. 三杯吐然诺，五岳倒为轻。　　　　　　　　　　——《侠客行》[唐] 李白

 Further Reading

1. *An Illustrated Book of Bad Arguments* by Ali Almossawi
2. *Fallacies: The Art of Mental Trickery and Manipulation* by Richard Paul and Linda Elder
3. *The Many Loves of Dobie Gillis* by Max Shulman

Unit 7
Style

Extensive Reading 4

Mastering Critical Reading

Language, as both a medium of communication and a carrier of arguments, is not an ornament to the reasoning, but an intrinsic component of an argument, shaping what the argument means, how it develops, and how people will respond to it. With careful arrangement, language can guide the audience's attention toward desired elements, thus enhancing the potential for acceptance of the argument's substance.

The presentation of arguments can vary significantly, depending largely on the selection and arrangement of vocabulary, sentence structure, and rhetorical devices; therefore, understanding how these elements function is especially helpful in discerning how an argument will proceed and formulating an appropriate response. Careful writers often choose appropriate language symbols to convey their desired message and, at the same time, to direct readers to decode the message as they encode it. The choice of words, sentence arrangement, use of rhetorical devices, and specific textual arrangements can all provide the audience with a rational basis for interpretation and evaluation. Critical readers need to think not only about what is presented but also about how it is delivered, keeping alert to implications and subtleties.

(Source: https://www.elttila.com/article/communication-style)

■ **Diction**

Word choice plays a significant role in constructing the style of an argument. The *level of diction* can directly impress readers with the formality of the whole writing and signal the seriousness of the writer. Are the words chosen primarily conversational or formal? Does the author employ slang words or technical terms? For academic arguments, a formal style is typically appropriate. These arguments usually choose incisive vocabulary and technical language to communicate with a serious audience. While everyday language or informal language can foster a more personal connection with the audience, an overabundance of colloquialisms or slang may lead to confusion and reduce the credibility of the substance they carry. Similarly, jargon, or vocabulary specific to a particular field, can distance or perplex an outside audience.

Besides the level of diction, an examination of word choice also involves *connotations*—the associated or implied meaning of a word beyond its literal or explicit meaning. A word's connotation is what the word suggests and what associations it evokes. Although some words may share similar denotations, or literal meanings, they cannot always be substituted for one another without slanting the message. For example, the words "house" and "home" both refer to a building in which people live, but the word "home" suggests feelings of family, warmth, and security, so it has a strong positive connotation. "House", by contrast, is more neutral, not bearing any such "emotional baggage" since it brings to mind only a picture of a physical structure.

> **?** Give at least two synonyms with different connotations for each of the following words.
> - thin
> - clever
> - well-known

■ Sentence Patterns

Usually, the *types of sentences* used in writing can reveal much about the relationships among the ideas they convey. A simple sentence often presents one piece of information independently, and a compound sentence usually carries pieces of information that are roughly equivalent in importance. Complex sentences display hierarchical relationships between points in main clauses and those in subordinate ones, while compound-complex sentences interweave more intricately related messages. Diverse sentence structures not only help readers grasp different relationships among the ideas, but also prevent the monotony and tediousness of uniform sentence construction. Additionally, the omission of some sentence elements or the inversion of them can be more effective in drawing the audience's attention to the target message.

In the same sense, sentences that vary in *length* also impress the audience differently. Writing that consists mostly of long sentences may appear formal but risks losing the audience's attention and patience, while writing that is dominated by short sentences can sound curt and thus weaken its credibility. Varying sentence length will function similarly to that of sentence types, infusing interest and navigating attention.

■ Rhetorical Devices

Rhetorical devices employ language in special ways for emphasis and variety. Some devices mainly play on the meanings of words or phrases, such as metaphor and hyperbole, while some devices make delicate arrangements of sentences, like parallelism and antithesis. Whatever means they take, rhetorical devices will not enhance the logical persuasiveness of the arguments, but they can make the writing more engaging and hence facilitate acceptance from the audience. The following are some often-read rhetorical devices.

❖ *Metaphor* and *simile* both draw a comparison between two dissimilar things. While simile creates explicit comparison with the express use of "like" or "as", metaphor makes implicit comparison without such signal words. These figures of speech are prevalent across various forms of writing and speech, particularly useful for illustrating abstract concepts with concrete imagery.

E.g. If music be the food of love, play on. (William Shakespeare)

Life is like a box of chocolates. You never know what you're going to get. (Forrest Gump)

❖ *Hyperbole* is a rhetorical device that creates a magnified effect through intentional exaggeration. It is often an obviously overstated or exaggerated statement targeted at emphasizing instead of being received as literally true. Conversely, an *understatement* is an expression that sounds much less forceful than what is real. Writers or speakers often employ this device intentionally to tone down the magnitude, making a situation seem less important than it really is. Both devices are often used strategically for navigating attention and focus and for ironic, humorous, or sarcastic effects.

E.g. ... and I had not known you a month before I felt that you were the last man in the world whom I could ever be prevailed on to marry. (Jane Austen)

I have to have this operation. It isn't very serious. I have this tiny little tumor on the brain. (Jerome David Salinger)

❖ A *paradox* is a statement that initially appears to be self-contradictory but makes sense upon further examination. This device is commonly used to challenge the audience to ruminate on and uncover the underlying logic within what seems to be a contradictory assertion. In the end, paradox invites readers to engage with the material in a unique way, allowing them to grasp the intended message through an unexpected perspective.

E.g. I must be cruel, only to be kind. (William Shakespeare)

Life is far too important a thing ever to talk seriously about. (Oscar Wilde)

❖ *Parallelism* is the repetition of grammatical structures, where two or more elements within a sentence or series of sentences mirror each other in form. This technique not only affects the grammatical architecture of the language but can also influence the interpretation of the ideas being presented. The parallel elements can be employed to emphasize or elaborate on an idea, or simply to intensify the rhythm and flow of the language.

E.g. ... and that government of the people, by the people, for the people shall not perish from the earth. (Abraham Lincoln)

I came, I saw, I conquered. (Julius Caesar)

- *Antithesis* juxtaposes directly opposing or contrasting ideas within a parallel grammatical framework. By pairing an idea with its opposite, antithesis clarifies the intended message through contrast. In addition, the parallel structure of antithesis also creates a repetitive pattern that reinforces the message, rendering it more compelling and impressive.

    E.g. *To err is human; to forgive, divine.* (Alexander Pope)

    ... ask not what your country can do for you—ask what you can do for your country. (John F. Kennedy)

- A *rhetorical question* is posed just for effect rather than to elicit a response, as the answer is either self-evident or not expected. Typically, a rhetorical question is asked when the questioner knows the answer himself and will share it, or an answer is not actually demanded. Such a question is often used as an impressive persuasive device to underscore a point or capture the audience's attention.

    E. g. *But is this a logical assertion? Isn't this like condemning a robbed man because his possession of money precipitated the evil act of robbery? Isn't this like condemning Socrates because his unswerving commitment to truth and his philosophical inquiries precipitated the act by the misguided populace in which they made him drink hemlock? Isn't this like condemning Jesus because his unique God-consciousness and never-ceasing devotion to God's will precipitated the evil act of crucifixion?* (Martin Luther King Jr.)

■ **More Contributors**

Besides those conventional and typical stylistic elements, many other techniques also contribute their share, large or small, in shaping the overall style of a piece of writing. For example, the special use of punctuation may suggest the need for more attention to the marked points. When a word or phrase is placed within quotation marks, instead of indicating its being cited from elsewhere, it may signal the writer's intent to challenge its conventional meaning or validity within the given context. Capitalizing words not normally capitalized or italicizing words or phrases lends those expressions additional weight by drawing special attention with more eye-catching typing.

Different from punctuation and typography, which are more effective in exerting influence on style at the micro-level, textual organization of the material functions better on the overall style of a text. An argument supported mainly by scientific studies, research, and statistics looks more formal, academic, and serious than the one relying heavily on anecdotal evidence.

Enhancing Your Critical Reading

Analyze the elements of style and their respective effect in "The Gettysburg Address"[1] by Abraham Lincoln.

Four score and seven years ago our fathers brought forth on this continent, a new nation, conceived in

Extensive Reading 4

Liberty, and dedicated to the proposition that all men are created equal.

Now we are engaged in a great civil war, testing whether that nation, or any nation so conceived and so dedicated, can long endure. We are met on a great battle-field of that war. We have come to dedicate a portion of that field, as a final resting place for those who here gave their lives that that nation might live. It is altogether fitting and proper that we should do this.

But, in a larger sense, we can not dedicate—we can not consecrate—we can not hallow—this ground. The brave men, living and dead, who struggled here, have consecrated it, far above our poor power to add or detract. The world will little note, nor long remember what we say here, but it can never forget what they did here. It is for us the living, rather, to be dedicated here to the unfinished work which they who fought here have thus far so nobly advanced. It is rather for us to be here dedicated to the great task remaining before us—that from these honored dead we take increased devotion to that cause for which they gave the last full measure of devotion—that we here highly resolve that these dead shall not have died in vain— that this nation, under God, shall have a new birth of freedom—and that government of the people, by the people, for the people, shall not perish from the earth.

Diction	
Sentence Patterns	
Rhetorical Devices	

Notes

1. On November 19, 1863, American President Abraham Lincoln delivered **the Gettysburg Address**, one of the most famous speeches in American history, in a dedication ceremony for a new national cemetery near the Gettysburg battlefield. There are five slightly different drafts of the speech in Lincoln's handwriting known to exist, each named after the person who received the copy. This version, the Bliss copy, written at Colonel Alexander Bliss's request, is the last known copy and the only one signed and dated by Lincoln. Today it is on display at the Lincoln Room of the White House. All five copies are available at https://www.abrahamlincolnonline.org/lincoln/speeches/gettysburg.htm.

Unit 7 Style

Text A Why I Taught Myself to Procrastinate

Preparatory Work

Activity 1 Are You a Procrastinator?

(Source: https://www.healthcareitleaders.com/blog/10-strategies-help-stop-procrastinating/)

In recent years, procrastination, or "Tuoyanzheng" in Chinese, appears to be increasingly prevalent and draws more concern. Are you suffering from procrastination? Do you think it is a genuine illness or simply an undesirable habit? How would you define procrastination? What potential benefits and drawbacks might it have? What suggestions would you give to those who are struggling with procrastination to make a change?

Your Definition of Procrastination	
Possible Benefits of Procrastination	**Possible Drawbacks of Procrastination**
Suggestions to Make a Change	

Activity 2 What Is Your New Year's Resolution?

What is a New Year's resolution? Do you often make such resolutions?

What is the most recent resolution you've set for yourself? Have you achieved it?

Will you possibly make a resolution to procrastinate? Why or why not?

Extensive Reading 4

  Reading the Text

> Procrastination is popularly regarded as a trouble for many people as it reduces productivity and can lead to increased stress. However, to Adam Grant, the right type of procrastination might work the other way—enhancing one's creativity. Actually a pre-crastinator, Grant has even tried to learn to procrastinate. But is procrastination really so beneficial?

Why I Taught Myself to Procrastinate
Adam Grant[1]

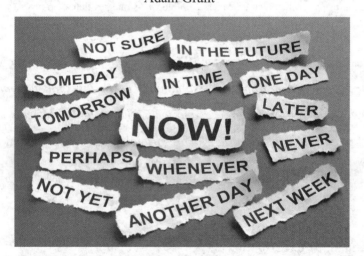

(Source: https://vidyasury.com/2015/01/15-ways-to-beat-procrastination.html)

1   Normally, I would have finished this column weeks ago. But I kept putting it off because my New Year's resolution is to procrastinate more.

2   I guess I owe you an explanation. Sooner or later.

3   We think of procrastination as a curse. Over 80 percent of college students are plagued by procrastination, requiring epic all-nighters to finish papers and prepare for tests. Roughly 20 percent of adults report being chronic procrastinators. We can only guess how much higher the estimate would be if more of them got around to filling out the survey.

4   But while procrastination is a vice for productivity, I've learned—against my natural inclinations—that it's a virtue for creativity.

5   For years, I believed that anything worth doing was worth doing early. In graduate school I submitted my dissertation two years in advance. In college, I wrote my papers weeks early and finished my thesis four months before the due date. My roommates joked that I had a productive form of obsessive-compulsive disorder. Psychologists have coined a term for my condition: pre-crastination.

6   Pre-crastination is the urge to start a task immediately and finish it as soon as possible. If you're a serious pre-crastinator, progress is like oxygen and postponement is agony. When a flurry of emails land in your inbox and you don't answer them instantly, you feel as if your life is spinning out of control. When you have a speech to give next month, each day you don't work on it brings a creeping sense of emptiness, like a dementor is sucking the joy from the air around you (look it up—now!).

7   In college, my idea of a productive day was to start writing at 7 a.m. and not leave my chair until dinnertime. I was chasing "flow", the mental state described by the psychologist Mihaly Csikszentmihalyi[2] in which you are so completely absorbed in a task that you lose a sense of time and place. I fell so deeply into that zone of concentration that my roommates once gave a party while I was writing and I didn't even notice.

8   But procrastinators, as the writer Tim Urban describes it on the blog Wait But Why, are at the mercy of an Instant Gratification Monkey who inhabits their brains, constantly asking questions like "Why would we ever use a computer for work when the Internet is sitting right there waiting to be played with?"

9   If you're a procrastinator, overcoming that monkey can require herculean amounts of willpower. But a pre-crastinator may need equal willpower to *not* work.

10   A few years ago, though, one of my most creative students, Jihae Shin, questioned my expeditious habits. She told me her most original ideas came to her after she procrastinated. I challenged her to prove it. She got access to a couple of companies, surveyed people on how often they procrastinated, and asked their supervisors to rate their creativity. Procrastinators earned significantly higher creativity scores than pre-crastinators like me.

11   I wasn't convinced. So Jihae, now a professor at the University of Wisconsin, designed some experiments. She asked people to come up with new business ideas. Some were randomly assigned to start right away. Others were given five minutes to first play Minesweeper or Solitaire. Everyone submitted their ideas, and independent raters rated how original they were. The procrastinators' ideas were 28 percent more creative.

12   Minesweeper is awesome, but it wasn't the driver of the effect. When people played games before being told about the task, there was no increase in creativity. It was only when they first learned about the task and then put it off that they considered more novel ideas. It turned out that procrastination encouraged divergent thinking.

13   Our first ideas, after all, are usually our most conventional. My senior thesis in college ended up

replicating a bunch of existing ideas instead of introducing new ones. When you procrastinate, you're more likely to let your mind wander. That gives you a better chance of stumbling onto the unusual and spotting unexpected patterns. Nearly a century ago, the psychologist Bluma Zeigarnik[3] found that people had a better memory for incomplete tasks than for complete ones. When we finish a project, we file it away. But when it's in limbo, it stays active in our minds.

14   Begrudgingly, I acknowledged that procrastination might help with everyday creativity. But monumental achievements are a different story, right?

15   Wrong. Steve Jobs procrastinated constantly, several of his collaborators have told me. Bill Clinton has been described as a "chronic procrastinator" who waits until the last minute to revise his speeches. Frank Lloyd Wright[4] spent almost a year procrastinating on a commission, to the point that his patron drove out and insisted that he produce a drawing on the spot. It became Fallingwater[5], his masterpiece. Aaron Sorkin[6], the screenwriter behind *Steve Jobs* and *The West Wing*, is known to put off writing until the last minute. When Katie Couric asked him about it, he replied, "You call it procrastination, I call it thinking."

(Source: https://reviewmybooks.co.in/procrastination-the-universal-best-friend/)

16   So what if creativity happens not in spite of procrastination, but because of it? I decided to give it a try. The good news is that I am no stranger to self-discipline. So I woke up one morning and wrote a to-do list for procrastinating more. Then I set out to achieve the goal of not making progress toward my goals. It didn't go excellently.

17   My first step was to delay creative tasks, starting with this article. I resisted the temptation to sit down and start typing, and instead waited. While procrastinating (i.e., thinking), I remembered an article I had read months earlier on pre-crastination. It dawned on me that I could use my own experiences as a pre-crastinator to set the stage for readers.

18   Next, I drew some inspiration from George Costanza on *Seinfeld*[7], who made it a habit to quit on a high note. When I started writing a sentence that felt good, I stopped in the middle of it and walked away. When

I returned to writing later that day, I was able to pick up where I had left the trail of thought. Mitch Albom, author of *Tuesdays With Morrie*, uses the same trick. "If you quit in the middle of a sentence, that's just great," he told me. "You can't wait to get back to it the next morning."

19 Once I did finish a draft, I put it away for three weeks. When I came back to it, I had enough distance to wonder, "What kind of idiot wrote this garbage?" and rewrote most of it. To my surprise, I had some fresh material at my disposal: During those three weeks, for example, a colleague had mentioned the fact that Mr. Sorkin was an avid procrastinator.

20 What I discovered was that in every creative project, there are moments that require thinking more laterally and, yes, more slowly. My natural need to finish early was a way of shutting down complicating thoughts that sent me whirling in new directions. I was avoiding the pain of divergent thinking—but I was also missing out on its rewards.

21 Of course, procrastination can go too far. Jihae randomly assigned a third group of people to wait until the last minute to begin their project. They weren't as creative either. They had to rush to implement the easiest idea instead of working out a novel one.

22 To curb that kind of destructive procrastination, science offers some useful guidance. First, imagine yourself failing spectacularly, and the ensuing frenzy of anxiety may jump-start your engine. Second, lower your standards for what counts as progress, and you will be less paralyzed by perfectionism. Carving out small windows of time can help, too: The psychologist Robert Boice helped graduate students overcome writer's block by teaching them to write for 15 minutes a day. My favorite step is pre-commitment: If you're passionate about gun control, go to the app stickK and fork over some cash in advance. If you don't meet your deadline, your money will be donated to the National Rifle Association. The fear of supporting a cause you despise can be a powerful motivator.

(Source: https://www.zoomly.co.uk/help-my-boss-is-a-procrastinator/vector-illustration-procrastination-businessman-which-delay-his/)

23 But if you're a procrastinator, next time you're wallowing in the dark playground of guilt and self-hatred over your failure to start a task, remember that the right kind of procrastination might make you more creative. And if you're a pre-crastinator like me, it may be worth mastering the discipline of forcing yourself to procrastinate. You can't be afraid of leaving your work un

(Source: This article was published in *The New York Times* on Jan. 16, 2016.)

Extensive Reading 4

Notes

1. **Adam Grant** is an American professor, bestselling author, and podcaster, who specializes in organizational psychology. He is a professor at the Wharton School of the University of Pennsylvania, and *The New York Times* bestselling author of 6 books. Grant also hosts the TED podcasts WorkLife and ReThinking.

2. **Mihaly Csikszentmihalyi** (1934-2021) was a Hungarian American psychologist, educator, public speaker, and the pioneering co-founder of the field of positive psychology. He is best known as the "father of flow"—a term he coined to refer to the psychological state of optimal performance, which he proposed in his 1990 book *Flow: The Psychology of Optimal Experience*.

3. **Bluma Zeigarnik** (1900-1988) was a Soviet psychologist of Lithuanian origin. She first observed and reported the tendency that interrupted tasks, in some circumstances, are recalled better than completed tasks, which is named after her as the Zeigarnik effect.

4. **Frank Lloyd Wright** (1867-1959) was an American architect, designer, and writer, widely viewed as the foremost American architect of the 20th century. He advanced organic architecture and designed more than a thousand buildings, many of which have become iconic such as Fallingwater, the Guggenheim Museum, and Unity Temple.

5. **Fallingwater** is a weekend residence in Pennsylvania that was designed by American architect Frank Lloyd Wright for the Kaufmann family in 1935 and completed in 1937. The house's daring construction over a waterfall grants it to be Wright's crowning achievement in organic architecture and the American Institute of Architects' "best all-time work of American architecture." Fallingwater opened as a museum in 1964, and was inscribed to the UNESCO World Heritage List in 2019.

6. **Aaron Sorkin** (1961-) is an American writer, producer, and director, best known for his screenwriting on political and news TV dramas. He pursued acting before realizing his passion and talent for writing. Sorkin has earned much acclaim for his writing for and producing many films and TV series, such as *A Few Good Men* (1992), *Moneyball* (2011), *Steve Jobs* (2015), *The Trial of the Chicago 7* (2020), *The West Wing* (1999-2006), *The Newsroom* (2012-2014), as well as *Molly's Game* (2017), his directorial debut. The film *The Social Network* (2010) won him an Academy Award for Best Adapted Screenplay.

7. **Seinfeld** is a popular American television situation comedy series in the 1990s about the misadventures of Jerry Seinfeld and his friends in New York City.

Unit 7 Style

 Remembering and Understanding

Answer the following questions.

1. What does the author think of procrastination? Is there any change in his opinion towards it?

2. What kind of person was the author, a procrastinator or a pre-crastinator? Why does he classify himself into that group?

3. What does the author mean by "progress is like oxygen" in Para. 6?

4. What is an "Instant Gratification Monkey" in Para. 8?

5. What requires great willpower from procrastinators and pre-crastinators respectively?

6. What do "it" and "the effect" mean respectively in the sentence "it wasn't the driver of the effect" in Para. 12? Why isn't it the driver of the effect? What is the driver of the effect then?

7. Was the author immediately convinced by Jihae Shin's experiments? What enhances his acceptance of procrastination as a virtue for creativity?

8. How does the author classify procrastination? What is the difference between those types of procrastination?

9. In which way are the guidance and experience offered in Para. 22 useful?

Extensive Reading 4

Reasoning and Analyzing

Answer the following questions.

1. What does the author imply by "normally" at the beginning of the text? What effect can it bring to the audience?

2. What can you infer about the attitude toward procrastination from the general public? What clues can you identify from the text?

3. What does the author intend to prove with the statistics in Para. 3? What do you think of the quality of the statistics and the author's use of them?

4. Why does the author ask readers to "look it up—now" at the end of Para. 6?

5. The author introduces the identity of Jihae Shin twice, first as one of his most creative students (Para. 10), and second as a professor at the University of Wisconsin (Para. 11). What effect would this introduction of Jihae Shin attribute?

6. Jihae Shin's experiments lead to the conclusion that "procrastination encouraged divergent thinking" (Para. 12). Are you convinced by this study? Why or why not?

7. At the beginning of Para. 16, the author raises a question—"what if creativity happens not in spite of procrastination, but because of it?" What do you think the author's conclusion to this issue is, in spite of it or because of it? Why?

8. How do you understand the ending of the article? How might the author feel about it? Why?

9. What are the features of the author's choice of words and use of sentences in the article? What effect do they bring?

10. What rhetorical devices does the author apply? What effect do they bring?

11. What would you conclude about the style of the article? What are the major contributors to this style?

Reflecting and Creating

Topics for discussion and writing.

1. In the text, the author provides a definition for pre-crastination, but not for procrastination. Why doesn't he give that definition? What would be his definition of it as used in this article? Summarize the definition for the author. What do you think of his intended definition? What do you think of his definition as compared with yours?

2. The author argues for the merits of procrastination in this article with different kinds of support. Are you convinced or is your previous opinion towards procrastination changed somewhat? If yes, what strikes you most in the text? If no, what other evidence or appeals are needed to render the argument more persuasive? Have you ever benefited from procrastination? Would you like to be a procrastinator?

3. As the article shows, sometimes a vice perceived from different angles may turn into a virtue. Think of your bad habits and pick one. Is it possible that this habit also bears some merits? Then choose one of your virtues and think about the situation in which it may bring trouble. If vices can bear merits and virtues are embedded with demerits, how can we decide whether it is a vice or a virtue?

Text B America Has a Love Affair with Exclamation Points!

Preparatory Work

(Source: https://sdtp.co.uk/harness-the-prowess-of-staying-in-the-game/)

What are your pet phrases? It seems that many people have their pet phrases—words or expressions that they frequently use, even subconsciously. Much like one's handwriting, pet phrases are believed by many to be revealing of one's character. Do you have pet phrases? If yes, what are they? Try to reflect on the expressions you like to use and share them with the class. What can you infer about their users from those phrases?

Pet Phrases in My Class	Possible Character of the Users

Reading the Text

As a relative newcomer to American English, the exclamation point enjoys a dramatic growth in its popularity. Although many writers have cautioned against its excessive use or suggested their reserved stance on the use of this punctuation mark, the exclamation point can be seen as an artful and innovative tool to express the American national eagerness for a better tomorrow.

America Has a Love Affair with Exclamation Points!

Ilan Stavans[1]

1   Crazy! Lol!! Super!!! In a nation of ecstasists that uses expressions like *great* to describe everything from a cup of coffee to a night's sleep, it isn't surprising that these cute punctuation marks—called "bang" "wonderer", and "screamer"—pop up just about everywhere to denote an unrestrained enthusiasm, though some see them as gendered expressions of emotion and others, mostly Gen Z, as passé.

2   It wasn't always this way.

3   We got the exclamation point from the British, along all things verbal. Yet the British are at a loss as to how they entered their parlance in the first place. Some argue, inconclusively, that they date back to the 18th century, derived from the Latin interjection *Iō!* ("hey!")," which medieval monks, through a process of decantation, redesigned by placing the o below the l, then shrinking it until it was just a dot.

4   The Hebrew Bible[2] doesn't use punctuation, so none are there. English-language translators, though, in their savvy creativity, have reversed the absence: the Revised Standard Version (Anglicized Edition) of the Old Testament has 1,087, and the New, 395.

5   "Alas! what harm doth appearance / When it is false in existence!", Geoffrey Chaucer utters in *The Canterbury Tales*[3], in order to display candor. And the exclamation point makes an appearance in Shakespeare's *First Folio*[4], although sparingly.

6   In the U.S., there are none in Francis Bellamy's "Pledge of Allegiance"[5], or in our sacred text, the Constitution. In 1828, Noah Webster[6], our unacknowledged Founding Father, who dreamed of American English as a language to homogenize the country through his groundbreaking *An American Dictionary of the English Language*, specifically defines exclamation as "outcry; noisy talk; clamor; as exclamations against abuses in government". He calls attention to the "emphatical utterance or outcry" that requires the mark, as in "thus!", yet avoids it at all cost.

7   In contrast, Emily Dickinson[7] used around 384 of them in her collected work, often to refer to "death-

conscious" experiences. In fact, possibly the very last poem, F338A, she is likely to have written ends with—surprise!—an exclamation point: "Good-by to the life I used to live/ And the world I used to know/ And kiss the hills for me, just once/ Now I am ready to go!"

8   Mark Twain[8] cautioned against their whooping perfidy in his 1895 essay "How To Tell A Story", as did F. Scott Fitzgerald[9], who said that using an exclamation mark is like "laughing at your own jokes".

9   Willa Cather[10] and William Faulkner[11] didn't shy away from incorporating them into a title (*O Pioneers!* and *Absalom, Absalom!*). Ernest Hemingway[12] includes a total of one in *The Old Man and the Sea*, which seems abnormal by today's standards. One example of its abundance in contemporary literature is Jennifer Egan's[13] novel *A Visit from the Goon Squad*, which features 108.

10   It is a cliché, of course, to disdain the exclamation point, but, as you might guess by now, I rather like it. And given its plenteousness, I can't be in the minority.

11   Still, William Strunk[14], in his classic *The Elements of Style*, states—stalely—that the mark is to be reserved solely "for after true exclamations and commands". Elmore Leonard[15], instead, settled, rather punctiliously, on a numerical approach: "You are allowed no more than two or three per 100,000 words of prose," he cautioned. Theodor Adorno[16] portrayed it as "a desperate written gesture that yearns in vain to transcend language".

12   Social media is the exclamation mark's natural habitat. Actually, a failure to use it while texting might be considered proof of psychological delayism, the syndrome of irremediably having fallen behind the times. Writing, at the top of an email, "Hi!" instead of "Hi," or, at the end of a message, "Thanks!" instead of "Thanks," suggests a kind of boredom, as life itself was colorless.

13   It might also be coupled with the question mark, yet "!?" isn't the same than a "?!": The first denotes puzzlement, while the second incredulity. Or is it the other way around? This pair has now merged into what is known as the interrobang. There is a persistence in usage of the interrobang from the 1950s to the present, a crescendo that feels, at least to the older generation, overwhelming. Mac and Google have created the combined "‽", which was created by advertising executive Martin K. Speckter.

14   And it likes to show up in groups. Whereas a period at the end of a sentence comes across as a demonstration of sarcasm, one lonely, unhinged exclamation point runs the risk of being interpreted as a manifestation of lukewarm affection. If it shows up in pairs, it is to indicate incredulity; three is proof of eagerness; four of fervor; five of out-of-control fondness; and more, stratospheric bewilderment.

15   Considering that the exclamation point is a relative newcomer to American English—it only got its own typewriter key in 1970—it is striking how much leeway it has made in our collective consciousness in such

short span of time. Just look around (when you happened to be offline): It shows up in road signs to invoke caution; commercial brands like Yahoo! and Chips Ahoy! use it to add a twist to their products; and it is ubiquitous in music lyrics, starting with The Beatle's "Help!" There is even a town in Ohio that changed its name to call attention to itself; it is now called, you guessed it, Hamilton!

16 It is also in countless children's books, from William Steig's[17] *Shrek!* to Dr. Seuss's[18] *Oh, the Places You'll Go!* And it is the domain of that most American form of entertainment for young and old audiences: the comic strip. No superhero worthy of their profession—bang! kaboom! and zap!—would dare to avoid it. Asks Superman, whose duty is to fight for truth, justice, and the American way of life. As he likes to say, "you can't throw morality in the garbage just because life's tough!"

17 What, then, has driven America to become so overtly exclamatory? As a nation of immigrants in which everyone strives to leave a mark, it is fair to say that we have always been an animated people that looks with anticipation to a better tomorrow. Yet unlike previous centuries, we now have more ways to voice that excitement, which in turn makes us look for more artful forms of linguistic exultation.

18 The history of the exclamation mark in English proves that punctuation, though frequently seen as constricting, is defined by innovation. Consider how zoomers, people born between the mid-1990s and 2010, have embraced lowercase. Or the fact that the semicolon, judging from social media, is a dinosaur, representing nothing, as Kurt Vonnegut argued, except to "show you've been to college". Punctuation is about how we perform before others; it isn't always appropriate to have good manners.

19 As for the exclamation point, yeah!, it continues to be a symptom of our national eagerness. Things might be difficult at times, but, wow!!, we can, with a simple expression, make it awesome!!!

(Source: This article was published on *Time* on Feb. 14, 2023.)

Notes

1. **Ilan Stavans** (1961-) is a Professor of Humanities, Latin American and Latino Culture at Amherst College, the publisher of Restless Books, and a consultant to the Oxford English Dictionary. He is also an internationally known, award-winning cultural critic, linguist, translator, public speaker, editor, short-story writer, and TV host, whose writing focuses on language, identity, politics, and history.
2. **Hebrew Bible** is the sacred writings of the Jewish people, comprising three main sections—the Torah (Teaching), the Nevi'im (Prophets), and the Ketuvim (Writings), most of which were written originally in Hebrew during the period from 1200 to 100 BCE.

Extensive Reading 4

3. **Geoffrey Chaucer** (c. 1342/43-1400) was an English poet and writer, widely considered one of the greatest English poets of the Middle Ages and the "father of English literature". Chaucer is best known for his *The Canterbury Tales*, a masterpiece of world literature, which is a collection of stories told by a group of pilgrims as they travel from London to Canterbury to visit the shrine of Saint Thomas Becket.

4. **William Shakespeare** (1564-1616) was an English poet, playwright, and actor of the Renaissance era. Known throughout the world, Shakespeare produced at least 37 plays, 154 sonnets, and 2 narrative poems. *First Folio*, produced in 1623, is the first published collection of William Shakespeare's plays, originally entitled *Mr. William Shakespeare's Comedies, Histories & Tragedies*. It contains 36 of Shakespeare's works and is the major source for contemporary texts of his plays.

5. **Francis Bellamy** (1855-1931) was an American editor and socialist minister, best known for writing the original version of "**Pledge of Allegiance**" (1892) although it has undergone several revisions.

6. **Noah Webster** (1758-1843) was an American lexicographer and writer, widely known for his *American Spelling Book* (1783) and ***American Dictionary of the English Language***, 2 vol. (1828; 2nd ed., 1840). The rights to the dictionary were sold in 1843 by the Webster estate to George and Charles Merriam, whose firm developed the Merriam-Webster dictionary series.

7. **Emily Dickinson** (1830-1886) was an American poet, best known for her frequent themes of death and mortality and her eccentric personality. Dickinson was a prolific writer, producing nearly 1,800 poems, although only 10 poems were published during her lifetime.

8. **Mark Twain**, born Samuel Langhorne Clemens (1835-1910), was an American novelist, humorist, journalist, and lecturer, known for his sharp wit and pithy commentary on society, politics, and the human condition. Mark Twain acquired international fame for his adventure stories of boyhood, especially *The Adventures of Tom Sawyer* (1876) and *Adventures of Huckleberry Finn* (1885), and his travelogues, especially *The Innocents Abroad* (1869), *Roughing It* (1872), and *Life on the Mississippi* (1883).

9. **Francis Scott Key Fitzgerald** (1896-1940) was an American novelist and short-story writer, famous for his depictions of the Jazz Age (the 1920s). His novels *The Great Gatsby* (1925) and *Tender Is the Night* (1934) become two keystones of modernist fiction.

10. **Willa Cather** (1873-1947) was an American novelist, acclaimed for her portrayals of the American pioneer experience, such as her novels ***O Pioneers!*** (1913), *The Song of the Lark* (1915), and *My Ántonia* (1918).

11. **William Faulkner** (1897-1962) was an American novelist and short-story writer, winner of the 1949 Nobel Prize for Literature. Faulkner is most noted for his novels set in the American South, frequently in fictional Yoknapatawpha County, including *The Sound and the Fury* (1929), *As I Lay Dying* (1930), and ***Absalom, Absalom!*** (1936)

12. **Ernest Hemingway** (1899-1961) was an American novelist and short-story writer, winner of the

1954 Nobel Prize for Literature, best noted for his simple and spare prose style. Hemingway was renowned for novels like *The Sun Also Rises* (1926), *A Farewell to Arms* (1929), *For Whom the Bell Tolls* (1940) and **The Old Man and the Sea** (1952).

13. **Jennifer Egan** (1962-) is an American novelist and short-story writer. Her novel, **A Visit From the Goon Squad**, won the 2011 Pulitzer Prize.

14. **William Strunk Jr.** (1869-1946) was a professor of English at Cornell University and author of **The Elements of Style** (1918). After revision and expansion by his former student E. B. White, the book *The Elements of Style* (1959) became a highly influential guide to English usage during the late 20th century.

15. **Elmore Leonard** (1925-2013) was an American writer of popular crime novels, known for his clean prose style, realistic dialogue, effective use of violence, satiric wit, and colorful characters.

16. **Theodor Wiesengrund Adorno** (1903-1969) was a German philosopher, social theorist, musicologist, and literary critic. Theodor Adorno was one key representatives of the first generation of the interdisciplinary and Marxist-oriented movement of thought called Critical Theory.

17. **William Steig** (1907-2003) was an American writer, illustrator, and cartoonist, called the "King of Cartoons" by Newsweek. William Steig is widely known for his 1990 book **Shrek!** which was adapted into film and won a 2001 Academy Award for best animated feature film.

18. **Theodor Seuss Geisel** (1904-1991), better known by his pen name **Dr. Seuss**, was an American writer and illustrator of children's books noted for their nonsense words, playful rhymes, and unusual creatures. Many of his books have become classics, such as *The Cat in the Hat* (1957), *How the Grinch Stole Christmas!* (1957), *Green Eggs and Ham* (1960), and **Oh, the Places You'll Go!** (1990).

Remembering and Understanding

Activity 1 Classify the People Listed

In the text, the author introduces the use of exclamation marks by some people or their attitudes towards it. According to him, some people are quite reserved and prudent in the use of exclamation points, while others are more supportive and encouraging. The following persons are all referred to in the text. Please classify them into different groups.

A. Geoffrey Chaucer	H. Willa Cather
B. Shakespeare	I. William Faulkner
C. Francis Bellamy	J. Ernest Hemingway
D. Noah Webster	K. Jennifer Egan
E. Emily Dickinson	L. William Strunk
F. Mark Twain	M. Elmore Leonard
G. F. Scott Fitzgerald	N. Theodor Adorno

Extensive Reading 4

Which group do they belong to?

Reserved and Prudent	Supportive and Encouraging

Activity 2 Answer the Following Questions

1. What do "these cute punctuation marks" in Para. 1 refer to?

2. How do people view these punctuation marks?

3. What is the possible origin of the exclamation point?

4. Why would Noah Webster compile that dictionary as suggested in Para. 6 and what is his opinion on the use of exclamation marks?

5. What does the author mean by naming it "a cliché" to disdain the exclamation point in Para. 10?

6. How would people in the age of social media regard one's failure to use exclamation marks?

7. What do the marks of "!?" and "?!" mean?

8. What's the difference between ending a sentence with a period and with an exclamation point or exclamation points?

9. How prevalent is the exclamation mark used in everyday life?

10. Why do Americans love to use exclamation marks so much?

Reasoning and Analyzing

Answer the following questions.

1. Why does the author begin his writing with "Crazy! Lol!! Super!!!"?

2. What point do the examples of Chaucer and Shakespeare illustrate?

3. What does the expression "surprise!" in Para. 7 indicate?

4. What would Fitzgerald mean by "laughing at your own jokes" in Para. 8?

5. What would William Strunk (Para. 11) think of the use of this mark? What does the author of this text think of Strunk's opinion? Why?

6. What would the author feel about the prevalence of the exclamation point in American English? Why?

7. What does the author think of the semicolon nowadays? What does he mean by the sentence "it isn't always appropriate to have good manners" (Para. 18)?

8. At the end of the text, the author states that "Things might be difficult at times, but, wow!!, we can, with a

Extensive Reading 4

simple expression, make it awesome!!!" How does this sentence function in the text?

_____

_____

9. What do you think of the style of this writing? How does the author achieve this style? Which approach is most impressive?

_____

_____

 Reflecting and Creating

Topics for discussion and writing.

1. In the discussion of style, we tend to lay more emphasis on an author's choice of words, arrangement of sentences, and application of rhetorical devices. How effective can punctuation be in affecting the style of a piece of writing? Pick out a paragraph or a short piece of writing by others, or write one by yourself, and then change some punctuation marks in the writing. How different are the two pieces of writing?

2. In this article, the author elaborates on American's increasing fondness for exclamation points. Have you observed any tendency in the use of punctuation marks among the Chinese? If yes, what is the favored or disfavored punctuation mark? Why is it favored or disfavored? If no, what do you think the reasons may be for exclamation points not being as popular in China as it is in America?

3. Similar to the exclamation mark as illustrated in the text, internet meme—an image, video, or piece of text, typically humorous in nature, that is copied and spread rapidly by internet users—enjoys tremendous popularity on various social networking platforms. What do you think are the similarities and differences between punctuation and memes in their affecting linguistic expression?

Summary

 Self-reflection

Fill out the checklist.

Area	Yes/No?	Notes/Comment
I know the power of language in argument.		

Unit 7 Style

(continued)

Area	Yes/No?	Notes/Comment
I know how diction contributes to the style of a text.		
I know how sentence arrangement contributes to the style of a text.		
I know some common rhetorical devices and how they contribute to the style of a text.		
I know the style of a text not merely relies on diction, sentence arrangement and rhetorical devices, but is influenced by more factors.		
I have a broader view about procrastination and precrastination, their possible merits and demerits.		
I have got a deeper understanding of the use of exclamation points and the functions of punctuation.		

 Value Cultivation

Activity 1 Message Identification

Which of the following statements would the author of Text A most likely agree with? Choose all that apply.

_____

A. Procrastination is the thief of time.　　　　　　　　　　　　　　　　—Edward Young

B. Procrastination is the art of keeping up with yesterday.　　　　　　　—Don Marquis

C. The interesting thing about overthinking and procrastination is sometimes they can actually evolve into innovation and creativity in the short term. Letting an idea grow in your mind in the short term with a deadline and a plan can actually lead to innovation and creativity.　　—Jay Shetty

D. Procrastination makes easy things hard, hard things harder.　　　　—Mason Cooley

E. Procrastination is like a credit card: it's a lot of fun until you get the bill.　—Christopher Parker

F. Procrastination comes in two types. Some of us procrastinate in order to pursue restful activities—spending time in bed, watching TV—while others delay difficult or unpleasant tasks in favor of those that are more fun.　　　　　　　　　　　　　　　　　　　　　　　　—Daniel Levitin

G. I try to procrastinate, if I can, productively, like I'll work on something else as procrastination. Or I take a walk. Because often I find, if you get out, more things come to you.　　—Noah Baumbach

Extensive Reading 4

Activity 2 Translate the Quotes or Poems

The following are some quotes or poems in Chinese culture and Western culture. Translate the English into Chinese and the Chinese into English.

1. Yesterday's the past, tomorrow's the future, but today is a gift. That's why it's called the present.

—Bil Keane

Chinese version: _____
_____

2. If you talk to a man in a language he understands, that goes to his head. If you talk to him in his language, that goes to his heart.　　—Nelson Mandela

Chinese version: _____
_____

3. 明日复明日，明日何其多！我生待明日，万事成蹉跎。

——《明日歌》［明］钱福

English version: _____
_____
_____

4. 子曰："质胜文则野，文胜质则史。文质彬彬，然后君子。"

——《论语·雍也》

English version: _____
_____
_____

Further Reading

1. 《习近平与大学生朋友们》，中国青年出版社，2020 年 11 月
2. *Think Again: The Power of Knowing What You Don't Know* by Adam Grant
3. *The Elements of Style* by William Strunk Jr. and E. B. White

Unit 8

Reading Literature Critically: Fiction

Extensive Reading 4

Mastering Critical Reading

Literature encompasses a broad range of written or spoken creations with imaginative, artistic, and intellectual value. Its essence lies in the skillful use of language to communicate ideas, evoke emotions, and capture human experiences. This expansive domain includes diverse literary forms such as novels, poems, plays, essays, short stories, and other works of literary merit. Literature exposes readers to various perspectives, ideas, and experiences, inviting them to engage in deep analysis and interpretation.

■ What Is Fiction?

Fiction, particularly novels and short stories, is the most widely embraced and popular form of literary works among readers. Through the power of storytelling, fiction captures the essence of human experiences, explores diverse themes, and stimulates imagination.

Fiction is a genre of literature that deals with imagined or invented narratives and characters. It is a form of storytelling that presents events, people, or settings that are not based on real or factual occurrences. Science fiction, mysteries, romance, fantasy, historical fiction, coming-of-age novels, and crime thrillers are all fiction genres. Essential elements of fiction include plot, characters, setting, theme, point of view, etc.

■ Elements of Fiction

1. Plot

When we read a story, we move from one scene of action to another. The series of cause-and-effect events that make up the story or narrative is the plot. There are five essential parts in a typical plot structure:

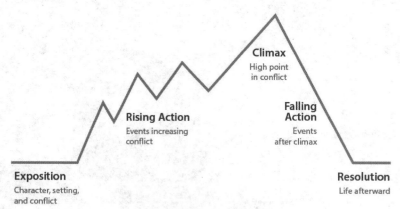

(Source: https://k12.thoughtfullearning.com/lessonplan/analyzing-plot)

The above diagram may help the reader understand not only how the main events in a story are generally organized into a plot but it is the conflict that creates and promotes the plot. Essential to plot, conflict refers to the struggle between opposing forces. There are two major types of conflict:

Internal conflict: This conflict arises within a character's mind or emotions. It involves their inner struggles, dilemmas, or moral choices.

External conflict: This refers to a struggle with a force outside one's self, including

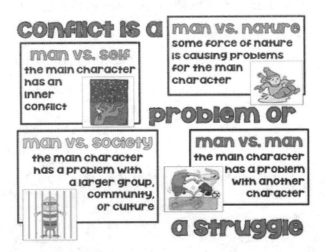

(Source: https://www.teacherspayteachers.com/Product/Conflict-in-Literature-1039711)

❖ *Character vs. Character*: This conflict occurs between two or more characters.

❖ *Character vs. Society*: The character faces a conflict with social norms, practices, rules, customs, or expectations.

❖ *Character vs. Nature*: The conflict arises between the character and natural elements such as weather, animals, or environmental challenges.

	What is the main conflict in *The Great Gatsby* by F. Scott Fitzgerald? How does it promote the development of the plot?

2. Setting

The setting of fiction refers to the time, place, and environment in which the story takes place. The setting helps to establish the backdrop for the story and influences the characters' actions, perceptions, and experiences. When considering the aspects of a setting, the following elements should be taken into account:

Elements of Setting	Meaning
Time	It refers to the era or time frame in which the story is set.
Place	It refers to the specific place where the story unfolds.

Extensive Reading 4

Elements of Setting	Meaning
Physical Environment	This means the natural surroundings, including landscapes, weather, geography, etc. and how they impact the characters and events.
Social and Cultural Setting	This encompasses the social structure, customs, traditions, values, and beliefs of the society or communities portrayed in the story.
Atmosphere and Mood	This refers to the emotional ambiance or overall feeling generated by the setting.

? When and where is *The Great Gatsby* set? How does the setting help establish the backdrop of the story?

3. Characters

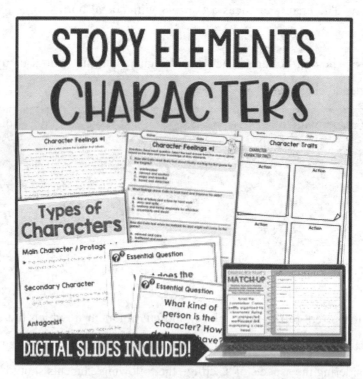

(Source: https://www.teacherspayteachers.com/Product/Describing-Character-Resources-Feelings-Character-Traits-MORE-w-Digital-9922115)

In fiction, a character is an individual or entity that is created by the author to play a role in the story. Characters can be human, non-human, or even abstract concepts personified.

204

In a work of fiction, the story usually revolves around the conflict between the **protagonist**, the central character, and the **antagonist**, a character who opposes the protagonist. Among these imaginary characters, some are **round**, displaying fully developed personalities or even contradictory traits that are affected by the story's events. Round characters often undergo significant growth or change throughout the story. Therefore, they are **dynamic**. In contrast, some characters are **flat** and less developed, exhibiting only a single characteristic or a few discernible traits. Flat characters often serve a specific purpose or function within the story and do not undergo substantial character development. Therefore, they are **static**.

To analyze a character, readers have to understand the process in which the author creates them, which usually encompasses the following devices:

Devices of Character Creation	Meaning
Physical Appearance	It provides important information such as the character's age, fitness level, grooming, and socioeconomic status about the character.
Speech	A character's speech may tell the reader something about the character's education level, geographical location, and attitudes.
Psychological Traits	Psychological traits embody a number of aspects that make up a whole person, among them thoughts, feelings, habits, and worldview.
Actions	A character's actions are what move the narrative of a story forward, creating and resolving conflicts, and establishing a story's sequence of events and rhythm.
Reactions of Others	What other characters say or how they respond to a particular character can provide insights into their personality, behavior, and impact on the story.
Author's own Opinion	On certain occasions, the author tells readers directly what the personality of a character is.

? What do you think Jay Gatsby is like?

Extensive Reading 4

(Source: https://www.weareteachers.com/point-of-view-videos/)

4. Point of View

The point of view (POV) in fiction refers to the perspective from which the story is narrated. It determines how readers experience the events and characters within the narrative.

There are several different types of points of view commonly used in fiction:

Types of Point of View	Meaning
First-Person	The story is narrated by a character who refers to themselves as "I" and is usually a participant in the events.
Third-Person Limited	The story is narrated from the perspective of an external narrator "he" or "she" who focuses on a single character's thoughts, feelings, and experiences.
Third-Person Omniscient	In this POV, an all-knowing narrator "he" or "she" has access to the thoughts, emotions, and experiences of multiple characters.
Second-Person	This POV is quite uncommon, where the narrative addresses the reader directly as "you."
Multi-person	Different chapters or sections in a story are narrated from the perspectives of various characters.

? What is the point of view of *The Great Gatsby*? Who is the narrator? How does the narrator's position in the story influence the reader's understanding of the events and characters in the novel? How reliable do you think of the narrator's account?

5. Theme

(Source: https://www.pandorapost.com/2021/06/literary-themes-examples.html)

The theme of a literary work is the core underlying message or idea that the author conveys through it. It explores the universal truths or insights about people, life, human nature, society, and the world that the author wants the reader to understand.

To uncover a theme, the reader must delve into the underlying narrative, which is conveyed through subtext, nuanced details, and unspoken events. By examining what lies beneath the surface, one can discern the deeper meaning and messages embedded within the text. The following strategies might be helpful in finding the theme of a story:

Identify the plot and central conflict.

❖ Are there conflicts between the main character and another, society or some force of nature, or within the main character him/herself?

❖ Figure out who or what the main character is struggling against in the story.

❖ Know how the conflict is resolved or why the conflict is unresolved.

Understand the main characters.

❖ Identify the protagonist and list the protagonist's friends and enemies.

❖ List the physical and intangible attributes of the main characters.

❖ Decide if the reader is supposed to identify with the main characters or if she/he is someone the reader doesn't (or shouldn't) want to be.

Pay attention to visual cues.

Search for recurring images, symbols or motifs throughout the story. These repetitions often carry symbolic, or thematic weight and can help unravel the deeper meaning of the narrative.

Extensive Reading 4

Examine the setting and context.

Pay attention to the story's setting, historical background, or societal context. These elements can contribute to the exploration of specific themes or shed light on the author's intention.

Reflect on the title.

Analyze the story's title as it can sometimes provide clues about the central theme or the author's intended focus.

Themes are subjective, and different readers may interpret them differently. The key is to support your interpretation with evidence from the story while considering the broader implications and messages conveyed by the author.

What are the themes explored in *The Great Gatsby*? How do the title, setting, conflict, and visual cues such as the green light and the parties help us discover the themes?

💡 Enhancing Your Critical Reading

Read the short passage below. It describes how a group of fifteen-year-olds were on a trip to Monos Island when a hurricane wrecked their boat. They managed to swim safely to a desert island.

1. **Roland** wiped his face.
2. "Indar and the boys get looking for food, and the rest of us will build some shelters."
3. Roland was the biggest in the group and was used to having his own way, but there were some grumblings.
4. **Tom** spoke up, "Says who? Nobody tells me what to do. I'll look after myself, that's all."
5. "If you were ill," said Indar, "you'd want someone else to look after you."
6. "Suppose I found the only bunch of bananas, you'd expect me to share it round, and not keep it all for myself? I don't want Roland to give me 'orders' but I do think we should share things."
7. "Right now, the most important thing is to find our way home," said Joe.
8. Tom disagreed. "The vital thing is to find FOOD," he replied.
9. "Look," shouted Ken. "Everyone is arguing. We need someone in charge to tell the others what to do. We need some guidance—some rules—else we'll be at each other's throats."
10. "I can do without rules," said **Lennox**. "You'll have us running round after you while you sit giving orders."

11. **Mitra** nodded in agreement. "Maybe we do need some rules," he said. "But I don't see that one person has to make them. Surely we should all agree what we need to do, then we can make sure things get done.

(Credit: *Social Studies for the Caribbean CXC Core Units and Options* by I. B. Beddoe, et. al)

Activity 1 Analyze the Characters

The characters in this story all have different views about how they should organize themselves to cope with the situation. What view does each of the following characters hold? Complete the following table.

Characters	View on Organizing Themselves on the Island	Evidence
Roland		
Tom		
Lennox		
Mitra		

Activity 2 Explore the Theme

Which of the following is the best statement of the theme of this story?

A. Collaborative resource-sharing and collective efforts are essential for the common good during hardships.

B. It is ethically wrong for one member of a group of to try to give orders to other members.

C. Teenagers are incapable of handling their own affairs.

D. Society can only work effectively if there are clearly agreed rules to which members conform.

Text A Lord of the Flies (Excerpt)

 Preparatory Work

Activity 1 Understanding the Plot of *Lord of the Flies*

The following is the sequence of main events in Lord of the Flies. *Drag each event to the appropriate point*

Extensive Reading 4

on the plot diagram.

1. A group of British schoolboys, aged 6-12, are stranded on an uninhabited island after a plane crash.
2. Ralph, one of the boys, is elected as the leader and he tries to establish order and create a signal fire to attract rescue.
3. Jack, another boy, becomes jealous of Ralph's leadership and starts to form his own group of hunters.
4. The boys struggle to survive on the island, facing challenges such as finding food and water, building shelters, and dealing with the fear of a supposed beast on the island.
5. The boys' behavior becomes increasingly savage and violent, with Jack's group becoming more dominant and Ralph's group losing control.
6. Simon, a boy who is kind and introspective, discovers that the supposed beast is actually a dead parachutist and tries to tell the others, but is mistaken for the beast and killed by the other boys.
7. Piggy, another boy who is rational and intellectual, is also killed by Jack's group, and Ralph is forced to flee and hide.
8. Ralph is hunted by Jack's group and is about to be killed, but is rescued by a naval officer who arrives on the island.
9. The naval officer is shocked by the boys' savage behavior and the destruction they have caused on the island.
10. The boys are rescued and taken back to civilization.

(Source: https://www.bydewey.com/lord.html)

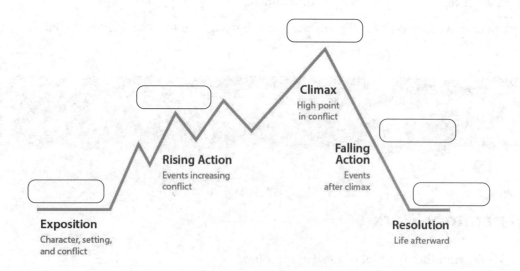

Activity 2 What Does the Title Symbolize?

(Source: https://gclt.com.au/lord-of-the-flies/)

The title "Lord of the Flies" is the name Simon has given to the severed pig's head that is placed onto a stake as a sacrifice for the beast, mostly because it is surrounded by flies when Simon sees it. What's more, "Lord of the Flies" is the literal translation of Beelzebub, a name derived from a Philistine god, and later mentioned in the New Testament, *in the Gospel of Matthew 12:24. Please explore its potential symbolism and significance based on the following questions:*

❖ What does Beelzebub refer to in religious texts?
❖ What do "Lord" and "flies" signify respectively in this context?
❖ What themes or ideas does the title suggest about the narrative?

Reading the Text

> Set on a deserted tropical island, *Lord of the Flies* explores the depths of human nature as a group of young boys struggle to survive and maintain order in the absence of civilization. As they face challenges and internal conflicts, the thin veil of society begins to crumble, revealing the primal instincts that lurk within us all.

Lord of the Flies[1]
(Excerpt)
William Golding[2]

[1] Once more that evening, Ralph had to adjust his values. Piggy could think. He could go step by step inside that fat head of his, only Piggy was no chief. But Piggy, for all his ludicrous body, had brains. Ralph was a specialist in thought now, and could recognize thought in another.

[2] The sun in his eyes reminded him how time was passing so he took the conch down from the tree and

examined the surface. Exposure to the air had bleached the yellow and pink to near-white, and transparency. Ralph felt a kind of affectionate reverence for the conch, even though he had fished the thing out of the lagoon himself. He faced the place of assembly and put the conch to his lips.

(Source: https://m.imdb.com/title/tt0100054/mediaviewer/rm132698369/)

3   The others were waiting for this and came straight away.

4   Those who were aware that a ship had passed the island while the fire was out were subdued by the thought of Ralph's anger; while those, including the littluns who did not know, were impressed by the general air of solemnity. The place of assembly filled quickly; Jack, Simon, Maurice, most of the hunters, on Ralph's right; the rest on the left, under the sun. Piggy came and stood outside the triangle. This indicated that he wished to listen, but would not speak; and Piggy intended it as a gesture of disapproval.

5   "The thing is: we need an assembly."

6   No one said anything but the faces turned to Ralph were intent. He flourished the conch. He had learnt as a practical business that fundamental statements like this had to be said at least twice, before everyone understood them. One had to sit, attracting all eyes to the conch, and drop words like heavy round stones among the little groups that crouched or squatted. He was searching his mind for simple words so that even the littluns would understand what the assembly was about. Later perhaps, practised debaters—Jack, Maurice, Piggy—would use their whole art to twist the meeting: but now at the beginning the subject of the debate must be laid out clearly.

(Source: https://clip.cafe/lord-of-the-flies-1990/the-reason-im-calling-assembly-is/)

7 "We need an assembly. Not for fun. Not for laughing and falling off the log"—the group of littluns on the twister giggled and looked at each other—"not for making jokes, or for"—he lifted the conch in an effort to find the compelling word—"for cleverness. Not for these things. But to put things straight."

8 He paused for a moment.

9 "I've been along. By myself I went, thinking what's what. I know what we need. An assembly to put things straight. And first of all, I'm speaking."

10 He paused for a moment and automatically pushed back his hair. Piggy tiptoed to the triangle, his ineffectual protest made, and joined the others.

11 Ralph went on.

12 "We have lots of assemblies. Everybody enjoys speaking and being together. We decide things. But they don't get done. We were going to have water brought from the stream and left in those coco-nut shells under fresh leaves. So it was, for a few days. Now there's no water. The shells are dry. People drink from the river."

13 There was a murmur of assent.

14 "Not that there's anything wrong with drinking from the river. I mean I'd sooner have water from that place—you know—the pool where the waterfall is—than out of an old coco-nut shell. Only we said we'd have the water brought. And not now. There were only two full shells there this afternoon."

15 He licked his lips.

16 "Then there's huts. Shelters."

17 The murmur swelled again and died away.

(Source: https://agbulordoftheflies.weebly.com/chapter-3-summary.html)

Extensive Reading 4

18 "You mostly sleep in shelters. To-night, except for Samneric up by the fire, you'll all sleep there. Who built the shelters?"

19 Clamour rose at once. Everyone had built the shelters. Ralph had to wave the conch once more.

20 "Wait a minute! I mean, who built all three? We all built the first one, four of us the second, and me 'n' Simon built the last one over there. That's why it's so tottery. No. Don't laugh. That shelter might fall down if the rain comes back. We'll need those shelters then."

21 He paused and cleared his throat.

22 "There's another thing. We chose those rocks right along beyond the bathing-pool as a lavatory. That was sensible too. The tide cleans the place up. You littluns know about that."

23 There were sniggers here and there and swift glances.

24 "Now people seem to use everywhere. Even near the shelters and the platform. You littluns, when you're eating fruit; if you're taken short—"

25 The assembly roared.

26 "I said if you're taken short you keep away from the fruit. That's dirty."

27 Laughter rose again.

28 "I said that's dirty."

29 He plucked at his stiff, grey shirt.

30 "That's really dirty. If you're taken short you go right along the beach to the rocks. See?"

31 Piggy held out his hands for the conch but Ralph shook his head. This speech was planned, point by point.

32 "We've all got to use the rocks again. This place is getting dirty." He paused. The assembly, sensing a crisis, was tensely expectant. "And then: about the fire."

33 Ralph let out his spare breath with a little gasp that was echoed by his audience. Jack started to chip a piece of wood with his knife and whispered something to Robert, who looked away.

34 "The fire is the most important thing on the island. How can we ever be rescued except by luck, if we don't keep a fire going? Is a fire too much for us to make?"

35 He flung out his arm.

36 "Look at us! How many are we? And yet we can't keep a fire going to make smoke. Don't you understand? Can't you see we ought to—ought to die before we let the fire out?"

37 There was a self-conscious giggling among the hunters. Ralph turned on them passionately.

38 "You hunters! You can laugh! But I tell you smoke is more important than the pig, however often you kill one. Do all of you see?" He spread his arms wide and turned to the whole triangle.

39 "We've got to make smoke up there—or die."

40 He paused, feeling for his next point.

41 "And another thing."

42 Someone called out.

43 "Too many things."

44 There came mutters of agreement. Ralph overrode them.

45 "And another thing. We nearly set the whole island on fire. And we waste time, rolling rocks, and making little cooking fires. Now I say this and make it a rule, because I'm chief. We won't have a fire anywhere but on the mountain. Ever."

46 There was a row immediately. Boys stood up and shouted and Ralph shouted back.

47 "Because if you want a fire to cook fish or crab, you can jolly well go up the mountain. That way we'll be certain."

48 Hands were reaching for the conch in the light of the setting sun. He held on and leapt on the trunk.

49 "All this I meant to say. Now I've said it. You voted me for chief. Now you do what I say."

50 They quieted, slowly, and at last were seated again. Ralph dropped down and spoke in his ordinary voice.

51 "So remember. The rocks are for a lavatory. Keep the fire going and smoke showing a signal. Don't take fire from the mountain. Take your food up there."

52 Jack stood up, scowling in the gloom, and held out his hands.

(Source: The excerpt in the text is taken from *Lord of the Flies* published by Penguin Books in 2003.)

Notes

1. ***Lord of the Flies*** is a novel written by British author William Golding, first published in 1954. The excerpt is taken from Chapter Five: Beast from Water.
2. **William Golding** (1911-1993) was an English novelist, playwright, and poet. He is best known for his debut novel *Lord of the Flies*, which established his reputation as a writer. In addition to *Lord of the Flies*, some of his other notable works include *The Inheritors, Pincher Martin, The Spire*, and *Rites of Passage*. He received numerous awards for his contributions to literature, including the Booker Prize in 1980 and the Nobel Prize in Literature in 1983.

Extensive Reading 4

Remembering and Understanding

Activity 1 Summarize the Main Idea

What is the excerpt mainly about? Summarize the gist of it in your own words.

Gist:

Activity 2 Identify and Synthesize Information

How are the following characters depicted in the excerpt? What can you learn about them? Complete the table.

Character	Brief Description
Ralph	
Piggy	
the littluns	
Simon	
the hunters	

Ralph mentions five problems that have arisen. What are they? Complete the table.

Problem	Brief Description

Unit 8 Reading Literature Critically: Fiction

Reasoning and Analyzing

Answer the following questions.

1. Conflict is the essence of a story. What are the main conflicts in the excerpt? How do the conflicts promote the development of the plot?

   _____
   _____

2. Ralph mentions five problems at the assembly as examples of one general problem which the children are facing. What do you think this general problem is?

   _____
   _____

3. What do you think these are meant to signify in the story?
   * the conch: _____
   * the triangle: _____
   * the fire: _____

4. Which of these words best sums up the style of government that the children appear to have adopted?

   A. Democracy.   B. Anarchy.
   C. Dictatorship.   D. Monarch.

5. Why isn't the style of government working very well?

   _____
   _____

6. Which style of government does Ralph seem to be advocating now?

   _____
   _____

7. Do you think the style of government Ralph is advocating will work? Give your reasons.

   _____
   _____

Extensive Reading 4

Reflecting and Creating

Activity 1 Evaluate the Children's Responses

When Ralph addresses the five problems in his speech, Golding describes very carefully the responses of the other children to each of the problems. Complete the table and evaluate the response by saying whether it represents agreement, disagreement, amusement, embarrassment, etc.

Ralph's Point	Other Children's Response	Evaluation
water		
shelters		
lavatory		
fire		
small fires		

Activity 2 Topics for Discussion and Writing

1. Writers rarely tell the reader directly what their theme is. Instead, they develop their writing in such a way as to enable readers to work it out for themselves. Could you write the theme explored in the excerpt in your own words?

2. Work out a dialogue between Ralph and one of the other characters, such as Piggy or Jack, in which they discuss their different perspectives on the importance of the fire.

Text B   The Oval Portrait

Preparatory Work

Gothic literature is a genre of fiction that emerged in the late 18th century. How much do you know about it? Do some research to fill out the missing information in the following box.

Unit 8 Reading Literature Critically: Fiction

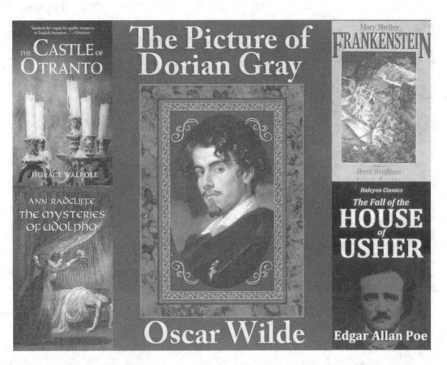

(Source: https://www.quora.com/What-are-the-primary-characteristics-of-gothic-literature)

Gothic Literature	
Definition	
Typical Elements	
Common Themes	
Major Authors and Their Representative Works	

Activity 2 Painting Analysis

Analyze the artwork, noting the colors, details, and emotions evoked. Then, relate your observations to the elements and themes commonly found in Gothic literature.

Extensive Reading 4

(Source: https://strongsenseofplace.com/2019/10/28/5-gothic-novels-that-feature-moody-houses-and-haunted-heroines/)

Get into small groups and have a discussion about the following questions:

❖ What are the predominant colors used in the painting?

❖ What is the effect created by the use of lighting and shadows in the painting?

❖ What are the prominent features of the architecture depicted in the painting?

❖ Are there any natural elements, such as clouds, bushes, or moonlight, depicted in the painting?

❖ How do these color choices, lighting techniques, and depiction of architecture and natural elements contribute to the overall mood or the atmosphere of the artwork?

❖ How do these elements and the overall mood of the painting reflect the themes commonly found in Gothic literature?

 Reading the Text

> Edgar Allan Poe, a master of Gothic fiction, weaves a haunting narrative in "The Oval Portrait". However, what makes Poe's best stories more than just gripping Gothic horror tales or unsettling stories is the way he clearly depicts a central idea, which the story explores and analyses. Undoubtedly, "The Oval Portrait" offers a fine example of this.

The Oval Portrait[1]
Edgar Allan Poe [2]

1 The chateau into which my valet had ventured to make forcible entrance, rather than permit me, in my

desperately wounded condition, to pass a night in the open air, was one of those piles of commingled gloom and grandeur which have so long frowned among the Appennines,³ not less in fact than in the fancy of Mrs. Radcliffe⁴. To all appearance it had been temporarily and very lately abandoned. We established ourselves in one of the smallest and least sumptuously furnished apartments. It lay in a remote turret of the building. Its decorations were rich, yet tattered and antique. Its walls were hung with tapestry and bedecked with manifold and multiform armorial trophies, together with an unusually great number of very spirited modern paintings in frames of rich golden arabesque.

(Source: https://karibribeiro.wordpress.com/hand-out-the-oval-portrait-by-edgar-allen-poe/)

2   In these paintings, which depended from the walls not only in their main surfaces, but in very many nooks which the bizarre architecture of the chateau rendered necessary—in these paintings my incipient delirium, perhaps, had caused me to take deep interest; so that I bade Pedro to close the heavy shutters of the room—since it was already night—to light the tongues of a tall candelabrum which stood by the head of my bed—and to throw open far and wide the fringed curtains of black velvet which enveloped the bed itself. I wished all this done that I might resign myself, if not to sleep, at least alternately to the contemplation of these pictures, and the perusal of a small volume which had been found upon the pillow, and which purported to criticize and describe them.

3   Long—long I read—and devoutly, devotedly I gazed. Rapidly and gloriously the hours flew by and the deep midnight came. The position of the candelabrum displeased me, and outreaching my hand with difficulty, rather than disturb my slumbering valet, I placed it so as to throw its rays more fully upon the book.

Extensive Reading 4

((Source: http://web.tiscali.it/manuel_ger/ill_ex/r_ovale_ill.htm))

4   But the action produced an effect altogether unanticipated. The rays of the numerous candles (for there were many) now fell within a niche of the room which had hitherto been thrown into deep shade by one of the bed-posts. I thus saw in vivid light a picture all unnoticed before. It was the portrait of a young girl just ripening into womanhood. I glanced at the painting hurriedly, and then closed my eyes. Why I did this was not at first apparent even to my own perception. But while my lids remained thus shut, I ran over in my mind my reason for so shutting them. It was an impulsive movement to gain time for thought—to make sure that my vision had not deceived me—to calm and subdue my fancy for a more sober and more certain gaze. In a very few moments I again looked fixedly at the painting.

5   That I now saw aright I could not and would not doubt; for the first flashing of the candles upon that canvas had seemed to dissipate the dreamy stupor which was stealing over my senses, and to startle me at once into waking life.

6   The portrait, I have already said, was that of a young girl. It was a mere head and shoulders, done in what is technically termed a vignette manner[5]; much in the style of the favorite heads of Sully[6]. The arms, the bosom, and even the ends of the radiant hair melted imperceptibly into the vague yet deep shadow which formed the back-ground of the whole. The frame was oval, richly gilded and filigreed in Moresque[7]. As a thing of art nothing could be more admirable than the painting itself. But it could have been neither the execution of the work, nor the immortal beauty of the countenance, which had so suddenly and so vehemently moved me. Least of all, could it have been that my fancy, shaken from its half slumber, had mistaken the head for that of a living person. I saw at once that the peculiarities of the design, of the vignetting, and of the frame, must have instantly dispelled such idea—must have prevented even its momentary entertainment. Thinking earnestly upon these points, I remained, for an hour perhaps, half sitting, half reclining, with my vision riveted upon the portrait. At length, satisfied with the true secret of its effect, I

fell back within the bed. I had found the spell of the picture in an absolute life-likeliness of expression, which, at first startling, finally confounded, subdued, and appalled me. With deep and reverent awe I replaced the candelabrum in its former position. The cause of my deep agitation being thus shut from view, I sought eagerly the volume which discussed the paintings and their histories. Turning to the number which designated the oval portrait, I there read the vague and quaint words which follow:

7 "She was a maiden of rarest beauty, and not more lovely than full of glee. And evil was the hour when she saw, and loved, and wedded the painter. He, passionate, studious, austere, and having already a bride in his Art; she a maiden of rarest beauty, and not more lovely than full of glee; all light and smiles, and frolicsome as the young fawn; loving and cherishing all things; hating only the Art which was her rival; dreading only the pallet and brushes and other untoward instruments which deprived her of the countenance of her lover. It was thus a terrible thing for this lady to hear the painter speak of his desire to portray even his young bride. But she was humble and obedient, and sat meekly for many weeks in the dark, high turret-chamber where the light dripped upon the pale canvas only from overhead. But he, the painter, took glory in his work, which went on from hour to hour, and from day to day. And he was a passionate, and wild, and moody man, who became lost

(Source: https://byronsmuse.wordpress.com/ 2021/10/07/arthur-rackhams-illustration-for-the-oval-portrait-by-edgar-allan-poe/))

in reveries; so that he would not see that the light which fell so ghastly in that lone turret withered the health and the spirits of his bride, who pined visibly to all but him. Yet she smiled on and still on, uncomplainingly, because she saw that the painter (who had high renown) took a fervid and burning pleasure in his task, and wrought day and night to depict her who so loved him, yet who grew daily more dispirited and weak. And in sooth some who beheld the portrait spoke of its resemblance in low words, as of a mighty marvel, and a proof not less of the power of the painter than of his deep love for her whom he depicted so surpassingly well. But at length, as the labor drew nearer to its conclusion, there were admitted none into the turret; for the painter had grown wild with the ardor of his work, and turned his eyes from canvas merely, even to regard the countenance of his wife. And he would not see that the tints which he spread upon the canvas were drawn from the cheeks of her who sat beside him. And when many weeks bad passed, and but little remained to do, save one brush upon the mouth and one tint upon the eye, the spirit of the lady again flickered up as the flame within the socket of the lamp. And then the brush was given, and then the tint was placed; and, for

Extensive Reading 4

one moment, the painter stood entranced before the work which he had wrought; but in the next, while he yet gazed, he grew tremulous and very pallid, and aghast, and crying with a loud voice, 'This is indeed Life itself!' turned suddenly to regard his beloved: —She was dead!

(Source: The story is on https://loa-shared.s3.us-west-2.amazonaws.com/static/pdf/Poe_Oval_Portrait.pdf)

Notes

1. **"The Oval Portrait"** is a horror short story by American writer Edgar Allan Poe, involving the disturbing circumstances of a portrait in a château. With the title "Life in Death", it was initially published in *Graham's Magazine* in April, 1842.

2. **Edgar Allan Poe** (1809-1849) was an American writer and poet known for his contributions to the genres of horror, mystery, and macabre. He is considered one of the pioneers of short stories in American literature and is most famous for his tales of the grotesque and the supernatural. Poe's works often explore themes of death, madness, and the human psyche. His notable works include *The Tell-Tale Heart, The Fall of the House of Usher, The Raven,* and *The Pit and the Pendulum.* His writing style is characterized by its dark and atmospheric tone, intricate plot structures, and vivid imagery.

3. **The Apennines,** or the Italian Peninsula, are a mountain range that consists of numerous peaks, valleys, and plateaus and extends down the length of Italy, forming the backbone of the country. They stretch approximately 1,200 kilometers (750 miles) from the northwest to the southern tip of Italy, parallel to the Mediterranean Sea.

4. **Mrs. Radcliffe** (Ann Radcliffe, 1764-1823) was an English author known for her influential contributions to the Gothic novel genre during the late 18th and early 19th centuries. She is often referred to as the "Mother of the Gothic" for her popularization of atmospheric and suspenseful storytelling. Radcliffe's most famous works include *The Mysteries of Udolpho* (1794) and *The Italian* (1797), both of which showcase her skill in creating suspenseful narratives set in exotic and mysterious European locations. Her novels were known for their intricate plots, vivid descriptions of landscapes, and emphasis on the psychological experiences of her heroines.

5. **A vignette manner,** in the context of painting, refers to a technique or style of creating a composition that focuses on a specific subject or element while allowing the surrounding areas to fade into the background. It involves creating a gradual transition from the focal point to the outer edges, often through the use of soft edges, fading colors, or subtle gradations. Vignettes are commonly used in portrait paintings, where the artist may focus on capturing the subject's face and gradually fade out the background.

Unit 8 Reading Literature Critically: Fiction

6. **Thomas Sully** (1783-1872) was born in England but immigrated to the United States with his family in 1792. He is considered one of the leading portrait painters of his time and made a significant impact on the art scene in both the United States and Europe. Sully's portraits are known for their naturalistic style, attention to detail, and ability to convey a sense of personality and individuality.
7. **Moresque** refers to a style of decorative art and design that originated in the Islamic world and later spread to Europe. It is characterized by intricate patterns and motifs inspired by Islamic art and architecture, particularly those influenced by the Moors of North Africa and the Iberian Peninsula.

Remembering and Understanding

Activity 1 Identify and Synthesize Information

At the beginning of the story, Poe gives a vivid description of the chateau where the narrator spends the night with his valet. Fill out the missing information about the chateau according to your understanding of the first paragraph.

The Mysterious Chateau	
Location	
Condition	
Characteristics of the Chateau	
Location of the Room Where the Narrator Stays	
Characteristics of the Room	

While the narrator lies in the bed, he is captivated by a portrait of a young girl. Fill out the missing information about the portrait according the author's description and account.

The Mysterious Portrait	
Identity	
Artistic Skill	
Frame and Decorations	

Extensive Reading 4

(continued)

The Mysterious Portrait	
Spell of the Portrait	
Story behind the Portrait	

Activity 2 Analyze the Main Characters

The following character map demonstrates the relationship between the four characters in the story. Try to find more traits of the three main characters based on the evidence in the text.

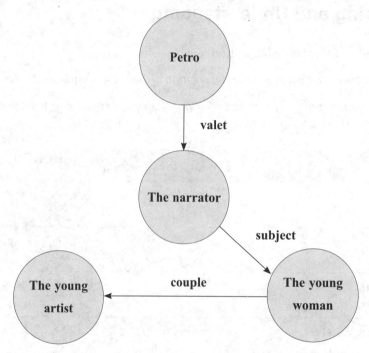

Characters	Traits of the Characters	Evidence
The Narrator	observant,	

Unit 8 Reading Literature Critically: Fiction

(continued)

Characters	Traits of the Characters	Evidence
The Young Woman	beautiful,	
The Painter	passionate,	

Reasoning and Analyzing

Activity 1 Multiple-choice Questions

Choose the best answer to complete the following statements based on the conflict presented in the story.

1. The main conflict in the story revolves around the _____.

    A. narrator's illness

    B. abandoned chateau

    C. mysterious painting

    D. marriage between the painter and his wife

2. The painter's wife is unhappy because _____.

    A. she dislikes the chateau

    B. she hates the artist's style of painting

    C. she is jealous of her husband's success

    D. She feels neglected and emotionally disregarded by her husband

3. The main conflict intensifies as _____.

    A. the narrator discovers the book about the paintings

    B. the health of the young girl deteriorates while being painted by her husband

    C. the young girl marries the painter

227

Extensive Reading 4

   D. the paintings in the chateau come to life

4. The climax of the story occurs when _____.

   A. the protagonist closes the curtains around the bed

   B. the painter finishes the portrait of his wife

   C. the painter realizes the painting is a true representation of his deceased wife

   D. the protagonist falls into a state of delirium

5. The resolution of the conflict is _____.

   A. unclear and leaves questions unanswered

   B. the death of the painter's wife

   C. the discovery of hidden treasures in the chateau

   D. the protagonist finding peace and leaving the chateau

Activity 2 Answer the Following Questions

1. How does the setting of the chateau contribute to the overall atmosphere and mood of the story? What effect does it have on the narrator's experience?

   _____
   _____

2. The oval portrait was hidden in the shadows and only revealed by the repositioning of the candelabrum. What does this reveal about the nature of the portrait?

   _____
   _____

3. Why did the narrator close his eyes after initially glancing at the portrait? What does this reveal about his emotional state and reaction to the painting?

   _____
   _____

4. What does "the cause of my deep agitation" in "the cause of my deep agitation being thus shut from view" (Para. 5) refer to? Why does it cause "my deep agitation"?

   _____
   _____

5. How does the relationship between the painter and his wife change throughout the story? What accounts for the change in their relationship?

   _____
   _____

6. What does the final line of the story, "This is indeed Life itself!" imply about the nature of art, the boundary between life and art, and the price paid for artistic perfection?
   _____
   _____

7. The chateau, the frame of oval shape and the candles are all important symbols that create the atmosphere, and theme of the story. What do you think they represent respectively?
   _____
   _____

8. Short as it is, "The Oval Portrait" is profound in several themes. What are some of the recurring themes that you notice in it?
   _____
   _____

Reflecting and Creating

Activity 1 Evaluate the Point of View of "The Oval Portrait"

Like many of Edgar Allan Poe's works, "The Oval Portrait" features a first-person narrator whose particular perspective frames and reinforces the main ideas and themes of the story. How reliable do you think the narrator is? Evaluate the point of view of the story based on the following questions:

1. How does the first-person point of view shape our understanding of the events in the story? What limitations or biases might be present due to the narrator's perspective?
2. In what ways does the narrator's point of view contribute to the atmosphere and overall mood of the story?
3. How does the narrator's personal involvement in the events affect his ability to provide an objective account? Are there any instances where the narrator's subjective interpretation of events might influence our understanding of the central themes?

Activity 2 Explore the Unresolved Ending of "The Oval Portrait"

1. "The Oval Portrait" ends abruptly at the climax without a follow-up paragraph telling the reader about the falling action and resolution of the story. Do you find the unresolved ending satisfying or unsatisfying? Why?
2. Write a follow-up paragraph exploring the painter's or the narrator's emotional state, thoughts, or actions in response to the young woman's death. Consider the Gothic elements and themes present in the story and how they can be further developed in the follow-up paragraph.

Extensive Reading 4

3. Share your paragraphs with the class and reflect on the different endings created. Do the follow-up paragraphs provide a satisfying resolution? How do you use your understanding of the Gothic elements and themes to shape the endings? Are there any recurring ideas or themes in them?

Summary

Self-reflection

Fill out the checklist.

Area	Yes/No?	Notes/Comment
I know the definition and essential elements of a fiction.		
I know the essential parts in a typical plot structure.		
I know the different types of conflict in creating and promoting the plot.		
I know the different aspects involved in understanding the setting of a fiction.		
I know different types of characters in a fiction and how to understand and analyze a character.		
I know different points of view in narrating a story and their different effects.		
I know how to explore the theme of a fiction step by step.		
I know how to evaluate the author's account critically.		

Unit 8 Reading Literature Critically: Fiction

 Value Cultivation

Interpret Key Concepts in Chinese Culture

"绘画六法" refers to the six techniques and aesthetic principles for painting formulated by Xie He, a painter of the Southern Qi and Liang dynasties. Please match the six techniques with their English equivalence and interpret them according to your understanding.

a. characteristic coloring
b. forceful brush strokes
c. imitation and copying models
d. dynamic style
e. life-like image
f. careful arrangement

1. 气韵生动
2. 骨法用笔
3. 应物象形
4. 随类赋彩
5. 经营位置
6. 传移模写

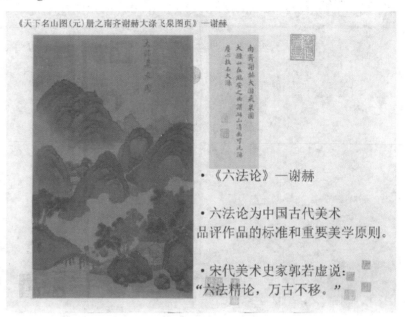

In *Experiences in Painting*, Guo Rouxu contends that "the six rules of painting are succinct and discerning and will stand the test of time. The latter five rules, starting with 'forceful brush strokes', can be learned. But 'dynamic style' requires innate aptitude and is not something that can be acquired just through scrupulous efforts or lengthy practice. Only an inspired mind can achieve dynamic style, yet without consciously knowing how". (*Key Concepts in Chinese Culture*, 2019)

❖ Do you agree with the author's assertion that "dynamic style" requires innate aptitude and, therefore, cannot be acquired through practice alone?

❖ What do you believe is the distinction between the five learnable rules and the rule of "dynamic style" in painting?

❖ How might this distinction impact artists' approach to their craft and the development of their artistic voice?

❖ What do you think the author means by "without consciously knowing how"?

❖ How might unconscious or intuitive elements contribute to the creation of dynamic style in painting or other forms of artistic expression?

Extensive Reading 4

 Further Reading

1.《发展社会主义民主——坚定对中国特色社会主义政治制度的自信》(《习近平谈治国理政第二卷》英文版)(2018)
2. *Lord of the Flies* by William Golding (1954)
3. *The Picture of Dorian Gray* by Oscar Wilde (1890)